LORD OF ARABIA

THE KEGAN PAUL ARABIA LIBRARY

ARABIA AND THE ISLES
HAROLD INGRAMS

STUDIES IN ISLAMIC MYSTICISM
REYNOLD A. NICHOLSON

A LITERARY HISTORY OF THE ARABS
REYNOLD A. NICHOLSON

LORD OF ARABIA: IBN SAUD
H.C. ARMSTRONG

LORD OF ARABIA
IBN SAUD

H.C. ARMSTRONG

THE KEGAN PAUL ARABIA LIBRARY
VOLUME FOUR

KEGAN PAUL INTERNATIONAL
London and New York

First published in 1934
This edition published by Kegan Paul International Limited in 1998
UK: P.O. Box 256, London WC1B 3SW, England
Tel: (0171) 580 5511 Fax: (0171) 436 0899
E-mail: books@keganpau.demon.co.uk
Internet: http://www.demon.co.uk/keganpaul/
USA: 562 West 113th Street, New York, NY, 10025, USA
Tel: (212) 666 1000 Fax: (212) 316 3100

Distributed by
John Wiley & Sons Ltd
Southern Cross Trading Estate
1 Oldlands Way, Bognor Regis
West Sussex, PO22 9SA, England
Tel: (01243) 779 777 Fax: (01243) 820 250

Columbia University Press
562 West 113th Street
New York, NY 10025. USA
Tel: (212) 666 1000 Fax: (212) 316 3100

© This edition Kegan Paul International, 1998

Printed in Great Britain by
Antony Rowe Ltd

All rights reserved. No part of this book may be reprinted or reproduced or utilized in any form or by any electronic, mechanical or other means, now known or hereafter invented, including photocopying and recording, or in any information storage or retrieval system, without permission in writing from the publishers.

ISBN 0 7103 0568 0

British Library Cataloguing in Publication Data
Armstrong, H.C.
  Lord of Arabia : Ibn Saud : an intimate study of a king. -
  (The Kegan Paul Arabia library ; v. 3)
  1. Abd al-Aziz, King of Saudi Arabia, 1876-1953 2. Saudi
  Arabia - Kings and rulers - Biography
  I. Title
  953.8'0099
  ISBN 0-7103-0568-0

Library of Congress Cataloging-in-Publication Data
Armstrong, H.C. (Harold Courtenay), 1891-1943.
  Lord of Arabia : Ibn Saud : an intimate study of a king / by H.C. Armstrong.
    p. cm. -- (The Kegan Paul Arabia library ; 3)
    ISBN 0-7103-0568-0 (alk. paper)
    1. Ibn Sa'ūd, King of Saudi Arabia, 1880-1953. 2. Saudi Arabic--
  Kings and rulers--Biography.
    I. Title. II. Series.
  DS244.53.A76 1997
  953.8'04'092--dc20   96-41813
  [B]   CIP

I DESIRE TO EXPRESS MY THANKS
TO
HIS MAJESTY KING ABDUL AZIZ
FOR
HIS HOSPITALITY AND MANY KINDNESSES
ON MY VISIT TO ARABIA

ACKNOWLEDGMENTS

I WISH to thank innumerable friends and acquaintances who have placed their personal knowledge at my disposal, but who must remain unnamed, and also:

>The British Museum,
>*The Daily Telegraph*,
>The Editor of the *Umu-al-Kura* of Mecca,
>The Imperial War Museum,
>The Royal Geographical Society,
>The Royal Institute of International Affairs,
>The School of Oriental Languages,
>*The Times*,

for placing much material in my hands and treating me with unfailing kindness.

H. C. A.

IBN SAUD

AUTHOR'S NOTE

TO describe, so that he may live before the reader, a Moslem and an Arab of outstanding personality, who is alive to-day, and who rules a great country, in terms that come within the everyday consciousness of Christians and Europeans has not been easy.

The Europeans and the Arabs have much on which they do not agree. They differ in experience, outlook, and manner of expression. Often their standards of right and wrong are not the same. Thus the desert Arabs are aghast at the unpunished adultery and fornication of the Europeans, while the Europeans are shocked at the legal polygamy of the desert Arabs. Polygamy is punished by imprisonment in Europe. Adultery is punished by death by stoning in Arabia.

I have, therefore, boldly translated both ideas and phrases, so that the reader shall grasp the correct meaning easily, rather than that his mind should boggle with uncertainty over meticulous details set down in unaccustomed language.

Arabic is full of complicated sounds which cannot be produced correctly with Roman characters. It has twenty-eight letters which can be made into intricate combinations and which change in shape as they combine.

For the spelling of Arabic words I have kept one rule that, while keeping as close to the sound as possible, the written word shall not torment the English reading eye. Thus Saud may be written Saoud, Sa'ud, Sa'oud, Seoud, Se'aoud, Si'oud, Esseoud, and in a dozen more ways. I have kept it as Saud,

Again an Arab delights in complicating names. Given any name he will quote a whole genealogical table for it. Thus he will describe Ibn Saud as Abdul Aziz ibn (son of) Abdur Rahman al-Feisal al (of the family of) Saud. He will add more generations if he is in the mood. To increase the complications he may call Ibn Saud, *Abu Turki*, the Father of Turki, Ibn Saud's firstborn son.

In this book I have for each personality chosen one name and retained it throughout.

On the life of Ibn Saud there is little documentary evidence, such as books and articles and records. The two principal authorities are Mr. St. John Philby, an English Moslem, who was at one time in the Indian Civil Service, and is now trading in Arabia for English and American firms, and Mr. Ameen Rihani, an Arab Christian from Syria of American nationality.

The major portion of the evidence collected has been from word of mouth. The books of Mr. St. John Philby and Mr. Ameen Rihani I have used freely. They are full of valuable material. I have, however, used them only after careful corroboration, whenever possible, with persons present at the events described.

INTRODUCTION

FAR back in Time, when Europe lay shrivelled and cold under the glaciers of the Age of Ice, Arabia was a land of forests and pastures, and watered by three great rivers.

Then as the earth spun over on its axis and its crust heaved, rising here and falling there, the seasons and the climates changed; and, as the ice melted, Europe woke to life.

But Arabia became a desert, for the rain came no more; the rivers dried up; the forests withered away; over the pastures swept shifting sand.

For many centuries it remained so. On its frontiers civilisations grew to maturity and decayed; countries became rich; great empires rose and fell. To the east along the banks of the Tigris and Euphrates rose Babylon and Nineveh; and beyond them Persia; to the west, Egypt and the Pharaohs with all their pomp and majesty; to the north, by the shores of the Mediterranean, Phoenicia and the Roman Empire.

But Arabia remained isolated and, except for rare travellers' tales, unknown. The merchants who came trading across the ocean from the Indies and Africa up the Red Sea, bringing jewels and ivory, spices and myrrh and frankincense to the trading-posts which the Jews had made at Mecca and Medina, told tales of great cities hidden behind the desert; but they were only travellers' tales. In the century before Christ the Emperor Augustus sent his Governor of Egypt to invade Arabia and find these cities. The Governor found only a barren land inhabited by wild tribes; and many of his men died of thirst in the great wastes.

Arabia remained isolated and unknown, for it was a brutal country and inhospitable, a land of cruelty and violence, and its inhabitants, the Arabs, were as brutal and cruel as their land. Where there was a little water, round wells, in an oasis, and on the sea-shores some built villages of mud huts, and with their primitive irrigation fought for existence against the sand that for ever came thrusting in on them persistent and relentless. The rest were shepherds, bedouin, who wandered throughout the seasons driving their flocks across the vast steppes in search of grazing.

Both villagers and bedouin lived hard and dangerously. They were pagans and savages, unclean, poverty-stricken, debased in their habits, idolaters with crude and brutal beliefs. They were bestial in sex, yet proud men, fiercely independent and prepared to sacrifice themselves for their freedom. Untamed and untamable, they were split up into small tribes, which were continuously at war with each other and were savagely intolerant of any stranger or of any innovation.

Suddenly out of this monstrous chaos was born a Great Man, preaching a Great Religion—the Prophet Mohamed preaching Islam.

Islam united the Arabs, purified them, bound them into one people. Mohamed filled them with a great Faith. His power increased rapidly. Within ten years he controlled all Arabia. His successors and followers advanced across the Euphrates into Persia and beyond. Northwards they went through Syria into Asia Minor and stormed at the walls of Constantinople. Westwards they swept along the African coast across the Sahara to the Atlantic and up into Spain and threatened France. Within a hundred years they had expanded their rule until the Arab Empire stretched from the Straits of Gibraltar to the Indus River and from Central Africa to the Persian frontier.

Islam itself went farther : to Constantinople and from there with the victorious Turks across the Balkans to the gates of Vienna to threaten all Christendom ; across the Black Sea to the Crimea and Russia ; and by Persia across Central Asia to the Great Wall of China.

But as the Arab Empire expanded and Islam became the Faith of many people, Arabia itself ceased to be the centre. The centre moved to Damascus, and then to Baghdad and Cairo. Out of the Desert had come the faith and the driving force, but Arabia, having given birth to these, sank back into its old state. Once more it became a land of ignorance and violence, shut off from the outside world.

Many more centuries passed. The Middle Ages, the Crusades, the Empire of Byzantium came and went. Tamerlaine the Tartar and Jengis Khan swept by, destroying. The Turks came conquering, seized and held all the gates to the East, and then in turn began to lose their grip and fail.

In all these events Arabia took no part. Shut away behind the barriers of the Desert, its people lived their own lives, strove with the sand for their bare existence, raided, murdered and fought each other in their eternal tribal wars and their bloodfeuds. The Turks claimed suzerainty over them, but it was without reality.

So a thousand years passed, and then once more, late in the eighteenth century, came a man with the fire of religion in him to weld the Arabs into one people and to inflame them into action. There came Mohamed ibn Abdul Wahab preaching a revival of Islam.

Ibn Abdul Wahab was a fanatic. He ripped away the heresies and abuses which had grown up round Islam and he preached the Faith in its original simplicity. He called on the Arabs to purify themselves, to forswear all pleasure and luxury, and with rigid asceticism to serve God, the One True God.

For a while he was persecuted, until he took refuge in the Principality of Nejd and claimed the protection of one Mohamed ibn Saud, who ruled in the towns of Dariya and Riad.

The centre of Arabia is a plateau shut in on three sides by desert and on the fourth by steppes where the bedouin graze their flocks. This plateau is the Principality of Nejd.

Over this plateau are scattered many villages and oases. The people of Nejd, the *Nejdis*, who live in them, are hardworking and stolid. Through the centre of the plateau runs a long valley rich in water and filled with palm-groves and gardens. In this valley stands the town of Riad.

Riad is the core of Nejd, and Nejd is the core and the very heart of Arabia. Who rules in Nejd may rule all Arabia.

Saud, the Amir of Dariya and Riad, was ambitious. He recognised the value of the Abdul Wahab. He made an agreement with him: together by preaching and the sword they would bring the Arabs back to the true Faith of Islam.

Their success was immediate. Saud was a leader and a soldier; Abdul Wahab was a preacher whose preaching caught the imagination of the desert Arabs. First they cleansed Dariya and Riad and then Nejd: they destroyed the idols and tombs of the saints; they enforced the orders of the Koran to the letter, the five daily prayers and the keeping of the Fast; they forbade smoking, drinking wine, and, as a dramatic warning, they stoned to death in the open market a woman guilty of adultery.

Tribe after tribe submitted to them and was filled with a

savage fanaticism. Their enemies nicknamed them *Wahabis*. Led by Saud, known as *the Great*, they swept out beyond Nejd conquering and coverting by the sword. Within sixty years they had established their rule across all Arabia, from the Persian Gulf to the sacred cities of Mecca and Medina and from the Indian Ocean to the Lebanon mountains of Syria. They were masters of the desert, and they refused to acknowledge the suzerainty of of the Caliph and Sultan of Stamboul and his Turks. They raided into Mesopotamia and destroyed the sacred city of Kerbela. With the hunger of desert-men for the wealth of the fertile lands beyond, and as their ancestors had done before them, they pressed on northwards to attack Syria and the shores of the Mediterranean, and so to burst out into the world beyond. They attacked Aleppo and made it pay tribute. They looted the outskirts of Damascus, and raided down to Basra.

The Turks woke to the danger. They ordered Mohamed Ali, their Viceroy in Egypt, to march into Arabia.

Mohamed Ali defeated the Wahabis, invaded Nejd, captured the Wahabi capital and sent the Wahabi ruler in chains to Constantinople. There before the Mosque of Santa Sophia where the Great Square runs down to the foot of the Bosphorus, the Turks beheaded him with much ceremony.

Then, weary of the harsh land, the Turks and Egyptians established a few garrisons and went gladly home, leaving the Arabs to themselves.

Like sand before the wind the Wahabi Empire of Saud the Great was gone. Nejd lay broken. With no strong man to unite and lead them, the Arabs split once more into quarrelling tribes. All Arabia was ripped into pieces by wars and raids, tribe raiding tribe while their sheiks plotted and intrigued, murdered their kinsfolk and rivals and were in turn murdered. Throughout the nineteenth century Arabia was again a land of bloodshed and strife, a land of brutality and violence where no man's life was safe and to which few travellers came.

Thus it was when, in 1880, on a November morning, at the time when the *mueddins* were calling to the dawn-prayer, there was born, in the palace at Riad, to Abdur Rahman, one of the descendants of Saud the Great and to Sarah his wife, a son whom they named Abdul Aziz, but who was known, after his great ancestor, as Ibn Saud.

PART I

LORD OF ARABIA

CHAPTER I

IBN SAUD was brought up in a wing of the palace. He was suckled by his mother, who was the daughter of one Ahmed Sudairi, a headman of the Dawasir tribe from the south. She was a big-built woman of a stock from which big men had come. Like all Arab women of good family she had been veiled since the age of seven and shut away indoors with the other women behind latticed windows and locked doors in the palace harem. She rarely went out, and then only heavily veiled, with a negro slave as escort, and to visit other women. Like other Arab women also, she had never been taught to read or write. Except for women's gossip she was ignorant of what went on in the outside world. She could neither be a companion nor take any part in the active lives of her men. But she had a shrewd judgment of values. She was devout, and with an innate common sense that made her wise in advice, so that at home she had much influence with her husband and her children.

The palace was an immense, sprawling building of halls and chambers and dark twisting corridors, built round a central courtyard and inside a high wall, but without plan. It had grown haphazardly. As more rooms were required, new houses had been built, connected into the rest by passages and overhead bridges, and the outer wall extended to take them in, until the palace filled all the centre of the town.

As soon as he was weaned, Ibn Saud was taken from the women's quarters and handed over to a negro slave who became responsible for him and his safety. As he grew up he often visited his mother, was petted and spoiled by her and the other women of the harem, and played with his elder sister Nura. But from that time on his place was with the men.

With him were brought up a number of slave boys of his own age, who were his companions until he grew up and then became his comrades and the most trusted of his body-guard. Almost as soon as he could walk his father, Abdur Rahman, took him in hand.

Abdur Rahman was both devout and strict. He was the Imam, the Leader, of the Wahabis. Their *ulema*, their Elders or Doctors of the Law, ruled them with a rod of iron. They were dour men, lean in body and outlook, who saw all life with the uncompromising eyes of the fanatic. They allowed themselves no luxury or even comfort. Their houses were bare and drab, their mosques without minarets, domes or any decorations. They refused all the pleasant things: wine, fine food, tobacco, soft clothes. They forbade singing and music and even frowned on laughter. They stamped out of life all joy, lest their thoughts might be led away from concentration on God. Their only indulgence was sex and their women. Their God was a stern God demanding absolute service of them. To those who served Him He was kind and merciful, but to the froward and unrepentent He was hard and merciless. They were His devoted people, lifted up over the heads of all mankind, with a mission to make all men His servants, even by the sword.

Abdur Rahman made no exceptions for his children. He brought them up as strict Wahabis. He sent Ibn Saud to school in Riad. The boy idled and played and showed no inclination for book-learning but, by the time he was seven, he was devoutly and regularly attending the public prayers with his father in the

Great Mosque five times a day, keeping the Fast, and could intone verses from the Koran.

Abdur Rahman had but one purpose in life. Either he, or, if he failed, his sons after him, must refound the Empire of Saud the Great, knit all Arabs into one people, and convert them into devout Wahabis.

He taught his sons that this was their duty : that this was a task for which God had chosen them. It would mean war, hardship, fighting. He prepared them for these. He taught Ibn Saud to use a sword and a rifle, to leap in one on to a horse and gallop without saddle or stirrups. To harden him to fatigue he sent him on long journeys. He made him rise regularly two hours before dawn, even in the winter mornings when the winds swept cold and bleak down from the plateau. He made him walk bare-footed at midday on the blistering rocks and the sand under the fierce summer sun. He encouraged him to test his strength, to wrestle and compete with other boys, and to ration himself in food, water and sleep.

Ibn Saud grew up rapidly into a lanky boy, tall and big-boned in contrast to his father who was short and thick-set. He was muscular and hard, full of energy, rarely still, and with a temper that flashed out like madness and died away as quickly as it came.

But he knew nothing beyond the narrow life of Riad. Behind the desert the town was shut off from the outside world. Its people were haughty as well as puritan. They despised and disliked all foreigners. Their only contacts with the outside world were the caravan merchants, who at rare intervals dared the trade-routes which ran through the empty deserts and were infested by bands of raiding bedouin; and who brought to Riad cloth and brass-work from Ojair and Kuwait on the Persian Gulf; or those from the Red Sea Coast who came with coffee from the Yemen, and with incense, spices and negro slaves from Africa, and who couched their camels and unloaded their bales in the open space before the palace and passed their news.

CHAPTER II

THOSE were days of danger and constant alarms. The country round the town of Riad itself was full of raiding parties of uncontrolled bedouin. Away to the north the Shammar tribes had united under one Mohamed ibn Rashid, a capable, ambitious man, who had made his capital in the town of Hail and who coveted Riad and the other rich villages of Nejd.

Riad was fortified. Round it ran a high wall, turreted, bastioned, and loopholed, along which sentries kept watch night and day. No one entered without being inspected and cross-questioned. At sundown and three times a day, when all the men were in the mosques at prayer, the iron-studded gates of the town were swung to and bolted against all comers.

The palace was a fort also, for Riad itself was torn with civil war. Abdur Rahman was one of four brothers. For ten years his elder brothers Abdullah and Saud had quarrelled and fought backwards and forwards for the mastery. Abdullah had driven out Saud, who had escaped and settled with the Ajman tribes who lived in the province known as the Hasa, to the east. Allied with the Ajmans he had raided back into Riad and driven out Abdullah. He died suddenly, and Abdullah returned, but the sons of Saud kept up the quarrel.

Between the two, the people of Riad were split into factions. They brawled and fought in the streets, and murdered and fought in the palace itself.

Abdur Rahman, together with his fourth brother, Mohamed, tried to act as peacemaker. He pleaded with both sides, warning them that the Rashid would take the first chance to attack them. He failed, for they were full of venom and threatened him as well

LORD OF ARABIA

so that he had to defend himself and his family in his own wing of the palace.

Finally the sons of Saud collected the Ajman tribesmen once more, took Riad, and imprisoned Abdullah.

FAMILY OF KING IBN SAUD

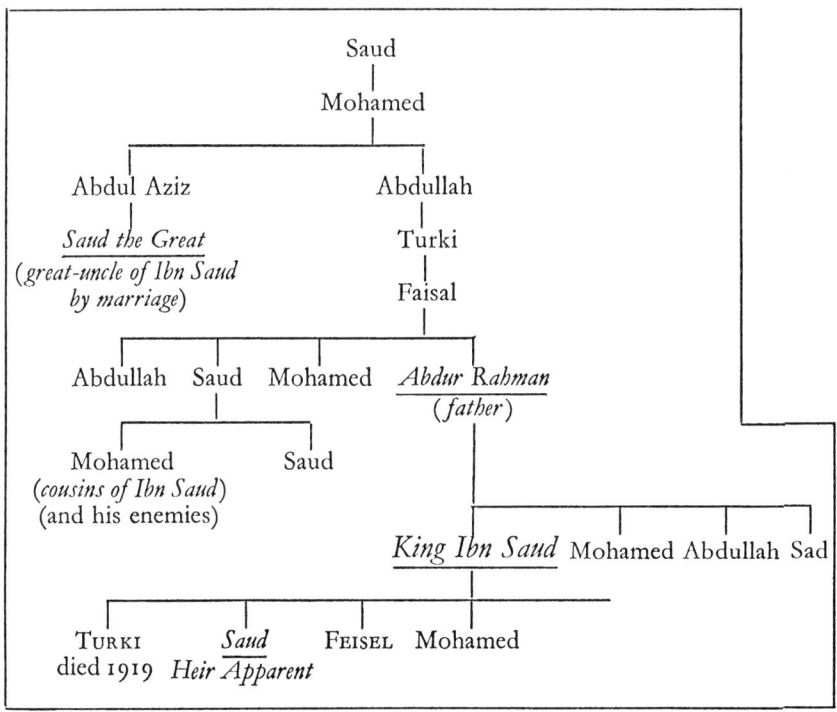

In the confusion the Rashid swooped down, captured Riad, drove out the sons of Saud, took Abdullah prisoner to Hail and put in his own governor, a sheik of the Shammar called Salim.

In the fighting Mohamed was killed by Obaid a cousin of the Rashid.

Abdur Rahman, because of his reputation as a peacemaker and because he had great influence with the Wahabis, the Rashid left in the palace with his family.

Abdullah fell sick. A Persian doctor, passing through Hail on his way to Mecca for the pilgrimage, was called in and warned the Rashid that Abdullah was dying. The Rashid, not wanting to be accused of murdering Abdullah, called Abdur Rahman to Hail and ordered him to take his brother back to Riad. Hardly had they arrived before Abdullah died.

CHAPTER III

ABDUR RAHMAN was now head of the family. Abdullah had been a poor, weak-kneed, sickly creature, but Abdur Rahman was proud and stout-hearted. He would not sit placid while Riad lay helpless in the hand of the foreigner. He meant to rule. He would chase the Rashid out and free the town.

He set to work without delay. He tried to come to terms with his nephews, the sons of his brother Saud, and get their help, but they refused: they treated him as an usurper: they claimed that they, and not he, had the right to leadership.

None the less he planned a rising in the town simultaneous with an attack from outside. He held secret meetings with the Nejdi leaders and urged them to rouse the townsfolk of Riad. He sent messengers through the villages and the tribes, but he met with little response. The people were afraid. There was a strong garrison of the Rashid's men in the fort which dominated the town. Once before they had risen and failed, and Salim had hanged and imprisoned many without mercy.

Abdur Rahman worked on undismayed. He was in constant danger. He was surrounded by spies and traitors, the enemy's spies and the confederates of his nephews, who would have betrayed him at the first opportunity to their common enemy.

Before he could make any effective preparations, however, the Rashid found out what he was at and sent orders to Salim to do away with him and to teach the town a lesson.

Salim decided to take drastic action. Once and for all he would be finished with these turbulent Sauds. They were all stiff-necked and quarrelsome. As long as any remained, there would be neither peace nor security in Riad. The Great Festival was coming to an end, and on the last day it was customary to make visits and exchange congratulations. He would pay Abdur Rahman a formal visit. He would take his guards with him and after he had talked for a while he would ask for the males of the Saud family to be called so that he might speak with them all. As soon as they were assembled his guards should surround and kill them.

But Abdur Rahman had news of this. Prepared or not, he would fight: better to be killed fighting than to have his throat cut without resistance. He armed such men as he had, and set them ready.

Salim arrived at the appointed hour, his guards round him, and Abdur Rahman received him in full state in the Audience Chamber of the Palace. To one side, so that Salim should have no suspicions, sat a few of the family, and among them, though still only a child, was Ibn Saud with his negro slave.

The two men exchanged greetings and congratulations full of fair words. With ceremony they performed all the courtesies, begged each other to be seated first, drank coffee together, talked pleasantly of trifles, while each hid what was in his mind as he watched the other and waited for the time to act—until Salim asked that the rest of the family might be called.

Then Abdur Rahman motioned to a slave and gave the arranged signal. His men came swarming into the Audience Chamber with their swords drawn. Overwhelming and killing his guards, they seized Salim and dragged him away.

Standing behind the huge negro slave who protected him, Ibn Saud for the first time saw blood shed in anger.

Immediately the whole town flared up, chased out the Rashid garrison, and prepared to resist. The villagers and the neighbouring tribes joined in.

The Rashid hurried down to crush the revolt, and Abdur Rahman went out to meet him. For weeks they fought in the desultory manner of the desert, a raid here, a skirmish there, but always Abdur Rahman was beaten back, until he was besieged in Riad. All the country round was in the hands of the Rashid.

As the weeks went by, food and water began to run short in the town. The enemy were cutting down the palms, destroying the irrigation channels and the wells, and making a desolation of the gardens. The townsfolk demanded that Abdur Rahman made terms. He refused. They threatened to rise against him. Forced at last, and very reluctantly, for he would have fought to the bitter end, he sent out a party with a flag of truce. With the party, as surety for his father, went the boy Ibn Saud.

They found the Rashid ready to treat. He wished to be gone: his men were deserting, tired of the drudgery of the siege, and there was no loot for them. He quickly agreed. As soon as Salim had been handed over to him uninjured, he appointed Abdur Rahman to act as his governor in Riad and then withdrew.

But, as he retired, the tribes rose against him, and Abdur Rahman collecting his men hurried out to join them.

With him he took Ibn Saud. The boy was now ten years old, and the time had come to blood him for war. Perched up on a camel, with his negro slave gripping on behind the saddle, he rode with the fighting men as they raided out after the Rashid.

But the Rashid turned. He smashed the tribes and came tearing back on Abdur Rahman. This time he would be finished with these vipers of Sauds.

CHAPTER IV

ABDUR RAHMAN could not stand for a fight. His men were a handful and afraid of the Rashid: they had begun to desert: the tribesmen who had joined him had already dispersed. He must make for Riad. To get behind its walls was his only chance.

Slinging Ibn Saud up into a saddle-bag on his camel, and almost alone except for his fighting slaves, he hurried back and prepared to defend the town. But the townsmen would not listen to him. They would not have another siege. It meant ruin for them. They wanted peace.

Close on his heels came the Rashid, swearing vengeance. Salim had been right, he said: the Sauds were a brood of snakes, treacherous, dangerous, not to be trusted; this time he would show them no mercy; he would wipe them out.

Late one night Abdur Rahman roused his family; they must be gone—and at once; they must run for safety; there was no time to spare; the Shammar scouts had been seen only a few miles away, coming down from the north; the enemy would be at the gates in a few hours. In the dark the women packed up into bundles all that they could carry, while the slaves carried the bundles out to the courtyard and roped them on to the camels. The women clambered up above the bundles. Ibn Saud and his brother Mohamed rode one camel, and before the dawn broke Abdur Rahman led the caravan out by the eastern gate of the town.

They travelled rapidly through the palm-groves and so into the Dahna Desert beyond, with scouts thrown out on the flanks to defend them against a sudden attack, and so came safely into the Hasa country. There Abdur Rahman claimed sanctuary with Hithlain the Sheik of the Ajman tribes.

The Ajman gave him protection—the code of the desert forced them to do that—but with a bad grace. The sons of Saud, who were living among them and intermarried with them, went through the encampments urging that the refugees be expelled. The Rashid demanded their surrender.

Abdur Rahman decided that there was no safety among the Ajman : they might turn on him at any moment. He distrusted them, for they were always treacherous and unstable. He arranged for his family to go to the Island of Bahrain, the Island of the Pearl Fishers, in the Persian Gulf. Ibn Saud had been ill with a type of rheumatic fever, and he sent him with the rest.

Then he turned to look for helpers to recover Riad. He refused to accept defeat, but none of the sheiks would ally with him. Collecting a few bedouin, who were always ready if there was promise of loot, he raided up to Riad, but the people of Nejd gave him no help, and he was easily driven off by the Rashid garrison.

As he returned, the Turkish Governor of the Hasa sent for him. The Turks were nominally the suzerain lords of all Arabia. In reality they held only the rich fringes, the Yemen, the Asir and the Hejaz on the Red Sea coast, with Syria on the north, and southwards by Mesopotamia down to Baghdad, and the provinces of Kuwait and of the Hasa, which ran along the western shore of the Persian Gulf and where they had garrisons in Hofuf, its capital, and in the other towns. In the interior and the inner desert they had no power or control.

Their policy was simple. Their object was to keep the tribes of the Interior from attacking them and from breaking out. To do this they played for a balance of power, setting one sheik against another, creating rivalries, helping the weak against the strong and supporting the defeated.

The complete defeat of the Sauds did not suit them, for the Rashid had become too strong and upset their calculations.

The Governor treated Abdur Rahman with great respect. He offered, with the help of regular Turkish troops and artillery, to send him back to rule Nejd, on condition that he accepted a Turkish garrison in Riad, acknowledged Turkish suzerainty, and paid tribute.

To this Abdur Rahman gave a blunt refusal. He was first and foremost an Arab and a Wahabi. The Turks were for him invaders and worse than infidels. He would not let them come interfering into Riad. He told them so without compromise, and they marked him down as a dangerous man. They remembered that twenty years before he had led a rising against them in the Hasa itself. At that moment there was trouble throughout the province: the Sheik of Qatar was known to be involved: Abdur Rahman had been visiting the sheik. The Turks suspected that he was behind the present trouble. They increased their garrisons and threatened both the sheik and Abdur Rahman.

With danger pressing on his heels, driven from pillar to post, a refugee, with the Rashid, the Ajman, with his nephews and the Turks after him, Abdur Rahman, taking with him Ibn Saud, who was now recovered of his fever, made southwards until he came to the palm oasis of Jabrin, and then on into the Great Waste, the Ruba al Khali, the Empty Quarter of Arabia, which stretched five hundred miles of empty desolation and sand down to the Indian Ocean.

By the salt-water wells of Khiran he found the encampments of the Murra tribesmen come out of the Great Waste to gaze their droves of camels in the low scrub. From them Abdur Rahman claimed protection.

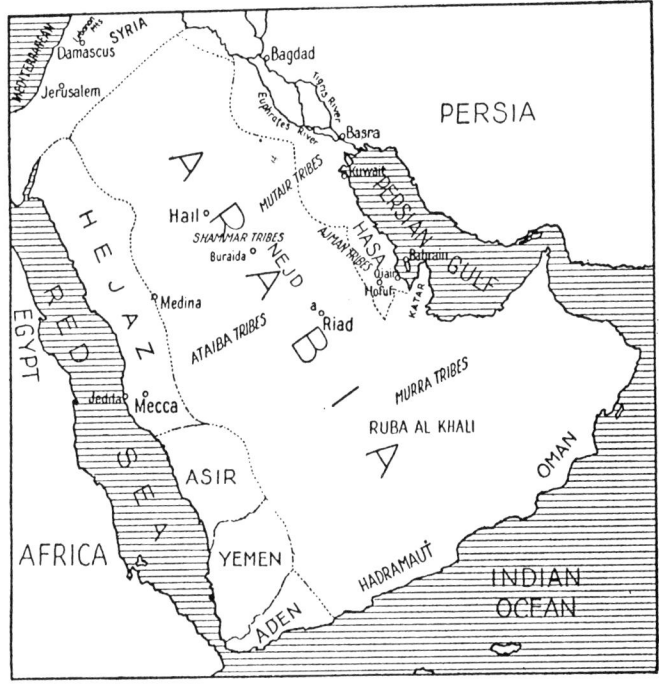

Map of Arabia in 1900.

CHAPTER V

FOR many months Ibn Saud lived with his father among the Murra tribes. With them were his younger brother, Mohamed, and his cousin, Jiluwi, a dark, saturnine youth, very dour in manner, who rarely spoke, but was always ready for any adventure. His mother and the women were safe in Bahrain.

The life was crude and brutal. The Murra were the most primitive of all the tribes of Arabia, long-haired, lean men with wild eyes and crafty faces. They lived almost as the animals and but little above the starvation line. Their food was a few dates gathered in the season at Jabrin and carefully rationed out to last the year, camels' milk—for the water of the wells of Khiran was salty and bitter and unfit for men to drink—and occasionally meat, when the hunters killed a gazelle, a sand deer, or a hare. More often their only meat was the *jabru* rats which lived in the rocks, and the tough horny *dhab* lizards, and sometimes a few ostrich eggs found in the sand—things not fit for the pious moslem to eat. Their greatest luxury was a little camels' liver rubbed in salt and eaten full of blood.

They had no villages. They moved continuously, driving their camels in search of scrub fodder. Wherever there was a little grass they went. They were the terror of all the other tribes, for without warning they would raid out of the Great Waste, killing and plundering, attacking caravans, and then race back into the safety of the vast waterless steppes where no one could follow them. They raided even as far as the Hadramaut, four hundred miles to the south, and stole the famous milch camels of the Terim and the red riding camels of Oman.

Among them Ibn Saud became the complete bedouin, living in the wide desert, often without a tent or any covering, under the open sky and the stars. He travelled with them, raided and hunted, and they taught him the ways of the desert: how to track by footmarks and the signs in the sand; how to handle camels on a long journey, doctor their pads and cure them of mange; how to travel distances with only a handful of dates and a skin of curdled milk.

From a boy he became an unkempt bedouin youth. The constant danger, the everlasting alarms, and the hardships toughened his body, and taught him reliance. It made him as lean as leather and at all times ready for action.

But for Abdur Rahman this life was purgatory. He despised the Murra. They were unclean, loose livers, worse than infidels; they were all but pagans with no religion. To be a refugee among them hurt his pride and roused all his religious indignation. At times he persuaded them to raid into the Rashid country, but the Rashid was too powerful for such raids to have any effect. Though he never lost heart and was for ever urging it on his sons, he saw little hope of attaining his great ambition or even of recovering Riad. He was getting old. He was over fifty and tired of this life. He wanted to get back where he could have his wives and his children round him. He sent messengers to many of the sheiks asking for protection, but without success, for he had many and powerful enemies and would be a danger.

At last, when he had all but given up hope, Mohamed, the Sheik of Kuwait sent him an invitation to visit Kuwait, and promised him a monthly allowance while he stayed there.

There had come to the Hasa a new Turkish Governor, Hafiz Pasha, who realised that he needed Abdur Rahman. The Rashid had grown so strong that he had become a menace both to the Turks and to Kuwait. Abdur Rahman would be the best counterpoise to the Rashid: he could use Saud against Rashid and so quiet the Rashid. Knowing Abdur Rahman's pride he agreed secretly with Mohamed of Kuwait to invite Abdur Rahman and his family, and he guaranteed Mohamed the allowance to keep them from the Turkish Government.

Abdur Rahman accepted the invitation gladly, collected his family from Bahrain, and with a sigh of tiredness settled in Kuwait.

PART II

CHAPTER VI

KUWAIT lay at the head of the Persian Gulf, an Arab town of sun-dried bricks of yellow clay and twisting alleys, crouching on a low shore—the houses coming down to a sandy beach and a shallow harbour protected by some primitive breakwaters. In the sunlight it lay a patch of staring yellow between the sea glare and the red desert that stretched away beyond it into the heat haze. There was not a garden nor a patch of green nor even a tree to rest the eye—except a few stunted tamarisk trees which fought with the sand.

The Sauds lived in a small one-storied house of three rooms grouped round a courtyard. The rooms were low, with windows of unglazed glass and heavily barred and shuttered. The roofs were flimsily built of thin rafters on which were laid palm-mats covered with beaten mud.

The street was a twisting alley that ran down to that end of the foreshore where the shipwrights and the sailmakers worked and where the pearl fishers hauled up and beached their boats. The filth of the town and the offal of the harbour covered the shore and stank under the sun and the flies.

The Sauds were crowded in their three rooms, for they were a large family. After the spacious palace at Riad, with its servants and slaves and the open life with the Murra, this drab town existence weighed heavily on them.

They were very poor. The Sheik rarely paid the allowance he had promised because the Turks rarely paid him, and though he was friendly he was also close-fisted and had no intention of supporting the Sauds. Eventually the allowance stopped altogether, for the Turks once more offered to send Abdur Rahman back to Riad with Turkish soldiers, and when he refused as bluntly as before they took no further interest in him. When Abdur Rahman heard from whence his allowance had come he was angry but was not able to repay it.

Often the family were short of food and clothes, so that Abdur Radman had to swallow his pride and borrow money.

When Ibn Saud was fifteen his mother found him a bedouin girl to marry, but when the time came Abdur Rahman had not the money for the celebrations, so the marriage was postponed until a rich merchant put up the money. This hurt Abdur Rahman's pride, but he accepted.

It was a dreary life, full of such humiliations: the empty, loafing, objectless life of exiles living under a cloud, not wanted, homesick for Riad with its clean air from the desert, and hating the dankness and the fever of the Gulf and the mud and stenches of the port.

In the town were many men of Nejd and Riad. A number lived in Kuwait as shopmen and traders. The rest came and went with caravans for the Interior or to man the pearling fleet when it set out for the season at Bahrain. They brought the news of Riad, but they brought no hope: the Rashid held the land in a firm grip: no one dared rise against him.

For Ibn Saud, Kuwait was full of new experiences. Hitherto all he had known had been the sour puritans of Riad and the brutal wild Murra of the Great Waste.

Kuwait was the Marseilles of the Persian Gulf. Its population was good-natured, mixed, and vicious. As it was the outlet from the north to the Gulf and hence to the Indies, merchants from Bombay and Teheran, Indians, Persians, Arabs from Aleppo and Damascus, Armenians, Turks and Jews, traders from all the East, and some Europeans came to it. From Kuwait the caravans set out for Central Arabia and for Syria.

Ibn Saud lived the ordinary life of an Arab youth. He loafed in the harbour and listened to the sailors. He sat on the edge of the cafés and sucked in the talk of the traders, the travellers, the sheiks in from the desert, and picked up the news of Baghdad, Damascus and Constantinople. He played knuckle-bones with the other youths in a corner, quarrelled and fought with them or went down the alleyways of the bazaars holding hands with his friends in the easy, intimate friendship of Arab with Arab, and played jokes on the shopmen until chased away. At the hour of prayer he joined his father in the mosque, and when the Fast came he kept it devoutly. The town was full of the vices of a seaport. Ibn Saud was intensely virile, but his puritan upbringing and his early marriage saved him from the harlots.

He was big-built for his age and very strong, with a quick wit and an open, frank manner.

CHAPTER VII

AMONG those who often visited Abdur Rahman was one Mubarak, the brother of Mohamed the Sheik of Kuwait.

Mubarak was on bad terms with his brother. Many years before, when he was still a young man, they had quarrelled, and Mubarak had gone to Bombay. There he had spent all his substance in gambling and riotous living. He had even sold his mother's jewels to pay his debts. He had lately returned penniless.

His brother still hated him. Being mean himself he hated his generous, free-handed ways. He was afraid of him too, for the people of the town liked him. He kept him short of money and humiliated him whenever possible.

Mubarak took a great liking to Ibn Saud. He treated him as a son, invited him often to his house, talked much to him, and taught him much worldly wisdom during these empty years of exile.

Suddenly, when Ibn Saud was seventeen, all was changed. Mubarak, stung into action by the humiliations and insults and being ambitious, crept one night with a cousin and an Ajman servant into the palace, murdered his brother, and made himself ruler of Kuwait. The people, tired of his skinflint brother, who had taxed them heavily and spent nothing on the town, accepted him gladly.

A few weeks later Mohamed ibn Rashid died. With wisdom and a strong hand he had ruled a great area from north of Hail down to the Great Waste south of Riad. His successor, Abdul Aziz ibn Rashid, was, however, no more than a filibustering chieftain out for loot. In a short time he had set all the tribes by the ears.

At once the Sauds became persons of importance: they were the friends of Mubarak; they were the enemies of the Rashid. Soon from Riad came messengers to say that the town was ready to rise, and that throughout Nejd the tribes were restless and would revolt if led.

Ibn Saud was in a fever to be off. He borrowed a camel, persuaded some friends to join him, and went raiding towards Riad. The messengers had been over-optimistic. The tribes did not rise. Mubarak gave no help, for he did not want a quarrel with the Rashid. Ibn Saud's camel was old and mangy. It went lame, fell, and refused to get up, and he was forced to start walking home until a passing caravan gave him a lift back on a baggage camel. All Kuwait laughed at the story.

Then, almost in a night, Kuwait became of world importance. For a generation Germany had been overcrowded with men and vitality. The Kaiser saw that she must expand or explode, and that the only road for expansion was to the East with India as the objective. But the English held all the roads to the East except the one that ran by Turkey through the Arab countries into the Persian Gulf. So the Kaiser allied with the Sultan of Turkey, proclaimed himself the friend of the Caliph of Islam and Protector of the Arabs, sent out his agents and pressed eastwards out of the West. As the backbone of his expansion he planned a railway from Constantinople through Aleppo down to Baghdad and with its terminus at Kuwait, for Kuwait held the door to the Persian Gulf.

For a century the English from India had been pressing up the Gulf from the East, allying with the local sheiks of the coast and so obtaining control. At Kuwait in 1897, the year that Mubarak became sheik, the two great World Powers came face to face, for the English were determined that the Germans should not come that way.

Mubarak listened to both. He received the consuls, and the representatives of England, Germany, and of Russia also, for the Russians, too, wanted a hand in the Gulf. He talked with secret agents of all sorts who came to him with offers.

He was shrewd. Position and power had changed him. He had ceased to be the wild, gambling, roystering spendthrift. He was as generous as ever, but he had become staid, steady, calculating, a crafty manipulator, an elusive diplomat and a strong ruler.

He knew what he wanted : he was nominally a subject of the Sultan ; but he was determined to keep Kuwait independent and for himself.

He saw that the English, like himself, were on the defensive and not out to annex, but that if the Germans with this railway came there would be an end of Kuwait. He played for time, giving nothing, postponing with empty promises, until the Germans, tired of this, eager to press on with the railway, urged the Turks to depose Mubarak. He was their subject, they said, he had murdered his brother and seized power : they had never recognised him : there was every justification for replacing him with someone more amenable.

Word of this came to Mubarak. Without delay he agreed with the English, and when the Turks threatened him they found the English behind him and were afraid to act.

Outmanœuvred, the Turks took a new line. They decided to rouse the Rashid to attack Mubarak. They would tell the Rashid that whoever ruled Central Arabia must have Kuwait : they would give him arms and money and promise him Kuwait, and he should agree to the railway : they would point out that Kuwait was full of his enemies, and that Mubarak was protecting his rivals, the Sauds. The English would have no valid reason for interfering between two Turkish subjects.

The Rashid, always ready for a fight, agreed at once and began to prepare.

CHAPTER VIII

MUBARAK saw his danger. He had no army : the people of Kuwait were not fighting men : even the town walls had been allowed to fall into ruins. He must find allies to meet the Rashid. He sent out messengers across the desert and found many of the tribes disgruntled. The Murra and the Ajman with the Mutair joined him, and then Sadun the Sheik of the Muntafik who lived up on the Basra frontier.

He looked on Abdur Rahman and Ibn Saud as important allies to be used to rouse Nejd when the time came, and he brought them into all his plans and conferences.

Abdur Rahman had, however, grown to disapprove of Mubarak. He had heard of his past life. He had learned that he was unorthodox in his manner of praying and, by Wahabi standards, his life was lax and immoral, for he had many foreign ways and habits. He wore fine clothes of silk. He prayed irregularly. He kept up a great state, riding through the bazaars in a carriage with black stallions and liveried coachmen, and ordering all to bend and salaam to him or be beaten by his guards. In his palace he had luxurious furniture, sofas covered with brocade, coloured windows, and pannelled ceilings inset with pictures of dancing girls. He received his guests and presided at his conferences seated in a gilded arm-chair like a European king. He smoked tobacco, and when he wanted entertainment he sent to Basra for dancing girls and musicians to amuse him.

All these things—dancing, music, tobacco, pictures, especially of women, luxury in clothes or furniture, and this haughty pomp —were anathema to Abdur Rahman. He would not go to the palace. He disapproved of Ibn Saud visiting Mubarak, so that

Ibn Saud, who went often, had to do so in secret without telling his father.

Mubarak however, developed a great affection for Ibn Saud. He encouraged him to visit him. He took him with him in his work, his audiences, and his conferences, and for Ibn Saud it was a fine schooling.

Of ordinary schooling, reading, writing and book-learning he had done none since he left Riad. But here with Mubarak he was surrounded by new ideas, new people, novel customs and ways of thought, many of which were forbidden and unknown in Riad. He met foreigners of all sorts, traders, merchants, travellers, representatives of the French, English, Russian, and German Governments. He saw how Mubarak handled them and how the problems of the outside world affected him. Moreover, Mubarak taught him much of the art of ruling.

To rule Kuwait was no easy task. The population came from all the tribes of Arabia. The caravan-followers were lawless. The pearl-fishers were the worst rapscallions in Arabia. The traders of all nationalities would cheat, quarrel, and brawl if he gave them the chance, but Mubarak knew how to deal with them. He was severe, and a dictator; his pomp was calculated to impress them. He did justice, quick and emphatic justice, to all alike. Under him in Kuwait there was absolute security of person and property, and the town prospered exceedingly.

Ibn Saud learnt quickly and readily. He was intelligent and shrewd and with a judgment beyond his years. Usually he was good-tempered and genial, but sometimes silent and depressed and with occasional bursts of wild anger.

When with his companions of his own age he often boasted, struck attitudes, telling them how he was the heir to Riad and Nejd: how he would one day chase out the Rashid and force the tribes and villages to accept him until he ruled the whole Empire of Saud the Great. His companions laughed at him, jeered at him, reminded him of his one attempt with the mangy camel that went lame. Their jeers made him angry, but they did not affect his belief in himself.

When with Mubarak he was always quiet and reserved. At audiences and conferences he would sit in a corner, his feet curled up under him, his brown Arab cloak drawn round him, playing steadily with the amber beads of a prayer-chain, but watching always, alert, absorbing all that happened, learning always.

CHAPTER IX

MUBARAK decided to strike before the Rashid was ready. He called up his allies. From Nejd came many volunteers. When he had collected 10,000 he marched out. With him he took Abdur Rahman, but he sent Ibn Saud south with a small force to rouse the country and create a diversion by attacking Riad.

Ibn Saud took with him Jiluwi his cousin and a number of men of Nejd from the town. Here was the chance he had hoped for. At last, after all these years, the tribes were rising against the Rashid. At the head of them he would smash the old enemy. He would prove to those who had laughed at him that he was not merely boasting. At last he was on the move, fighting and leading his own men.

Sweeping wide across the desert and travelling very fast he roused the villagers and the tribesmen of Nejd. They answered him gladly. They were tired of the Rashid, and they were overjoyed to see a Saud. They came swarming in to help him, so that by the time he reached Riad he had a large force.

Suddenly there came news from the north. Mubarak had found the Rashid before the village of Sarif. He had attacked. His allies had failed him. The Muntafik had bolted. The Ajman, as treacherous as ever, had left him in the lurch. He had been defeated. Only a sudden storm of rain had saved his army from being wiped out. He was retreating helter-skelter to Kuwait.

Ibn Saud's force broke up at the news. The tribesmen slunk home: the villagers bolted in panic: the fear of the Rashid was on them. Ibn Saud with a few men hurried back to Kuwait to find that Mubarak and his father were organising resistance.

After them came the Rashid, and as he came he burned the

villages of Nejd as punishment. In the town of Buraida he hanged 180 of the head-men and placed heavy fines on all. Having cowed the people back into submision, he turned on Kuwait, beat Mubarak's last troops at Jahra, a village close outside the town, and prepared to storm the town itself.

Mubarak was finished: he was without troops: his town unfortified: his allies dispersed: his confederacy broken up. Kuwait was all but in the hands of the enemy.

For the Sauds there was no hope: they could expect no mercy. Once more Abdur Rahman prepared to be up and away before the enemy came on them.

At that moment the English stepped in. Mubarak was their ally, they said. They warned the Rashid back. They sent a cruiser to enforce the warning. The Rashid halted and retired. Once more they had saved Mubarak and also shut this door to the East in the face of the Germans and their Turkish allies.

CHAPTER X

THE Rashid had defeated them, but Ibn Saud refused to accept defeat.

He was a man now, twenty years old, a great swaggering, rough bedouin buck, full of fire and spirit and spunk, spoiling for a fight, a giant of a man, a foot taller than the average Arab, and broad, with a big manner, and of great strength. He had brown eyes that usually were steady or smiling, but when he was roused were full of fire.

He cursed the Ajman : they were treacherous curs. He spat with fury at the news of the Rashid murdering his men in the villages round Riad. He blamed Mubarak for mishandling his army. He tried to rouse Mubarak to fight again, and when he failed looked for helpers among the neighbouring sheiks, but without success. They had all had their bellyful at Sarif. They would not stand up to the Rashid.

Abdur Rahman tried to dissuade him. The time was not yet. He had better wait. Later on they could organise something new.

But Ibn Saud refused to listen. Proud as Lucifer, he was afire to be up and doing. He had had enough of idling. For six years he had sat in Kuwait, loafing, eating out his heart, listening to the hopeless grumbles of the exiles. That was no life for a man. It might do for shopmen and clerks, but not for a Saud. He was a fighting man. This mooning café-life drove him to fury. He wanted action. To be up and out in the desert, with a camel or a horse between his knees. The desert was full of chances. With God's help he would win. He was sure of himself and of the people of Nejd. If he gave them the lead they would rise and join him and throw out the Rashid. Only he must have camels, money, and arms ; and he had none of these.

Week after week he argued with Mubarak, using all his persuasion. He approached the English representative in the town asking for help but got no reply. At last Mubarak gave way. After all it would be good to harry the Rashid and he could always disown Ibn Saud if it were necessary. So he gave him thirty camels, some of which were bitten with the mange, thirty rifles with ammunition, and 200 riyals in gold and let him go.

Ibn Saud wasted no time. Since his marriage he had lived in a separate house. His first wife, the little bedouin girl, had died six months after their marriage. He had taken two more wives, and by the first one he had a son whom he had called Turki. He arranged with his father that they should stay with him.

He quickly found thirty of his friends as eager as himself and ready to let him lead them. Jiluwi and his brother Mohamed joined him, and he distributed the arms and ammunition. Then he went to the house by the harbour and said good-bye to his family. His mother, like his father, would have persuaded him against going. With tears she begged him to wait awhile. She was sure he was going to his death or at least to ignominious failure, but his sister Nura urged him with every encouragement to act. She was as ambitious and turbulent as himself. Now that he was decided to go, Abdur Rahman gave him his blessing.

It was late summer when he started. One hot night before the moon was up he went silently and without advertising the fact, with his companions, through the twisting alleys to where the open market led to the encampments of the bedouin and then out into the country beyond to the rendezvous where the camels waited couched, with the slaves squatting beside them. A fighting man to a camel, the lurch of the rising camels, and they were away in the dark, making for the open desert.

CHAPTER XI

AT first Ibn Saud had success. He had learned from the Murra to move with speed. He allowed his men only a raider's kit, a blanket under the camel saddle, a rifle with ammunition, a handful of dates, and a bag of dried curds for a week's ration.

He knew how to cover his tracks and how to camp so as not to show against the skyline, in some hollow, the men in a circle, the camels hobbled and couched within the circle, and outside the sentries squatted, each with a camel saddle for cover and with rifle ready, watching for danger.

Working across the trackless sandhills he would come swooping down on to a caravan or a village, his men behind him yelling his battle-cry, raid, loot, and be away fifty miles by the following evening to raid again somewhere.

Nothing tired him. When the others slept exhausted, he was often away scouting out on his own. He slept little, just lying down, making a place for himself in the warm sand for an hour or two, and then up and on again.

He was in his element in a fight. He loved fighting, especially hand to hand. Bellowing like a bull he would come racing into a crowd, towering above them, hacking and laying about him with his sword, scattering them this way and that with his great strength, so that no man dared to face him. He inspired his men with his own energy and courage.

Skirting down the Hasa he first raided an Ajman and then a Rashid encampment and found good loot. News of his success went out, and, as he had gold and was liberal-handed, the bedouin joined him in numbers, and he harried the allies of the Rashid half across Arabia.

But he had not come raiding just for loot or the intoxication of fighting. He was not a common freebooter. He knew the bedouin themselves were of little value to him. He had come out to rouse his people of Nejd and Riad to revolt against the Rashid.

But they did not rise. They had risen when he had come in the previous year. They had made a mistake and they had suffered. Ibn Saud must prove his worth before they would rise again.

Then came a lean time : Ibn Saud's raids failed ; his money came to an end ; his camels were overworked and in poor condition ; his ammunition was getting short ; the bedouin, seeing neither gold nor loot, deserted him ; the Rashid sent men to Nejd who chased him out. He turned into the Hasa and was chased from there by the Ajman and by the Turks who pressed Mubarak to recall him. Cursing the Ajman and the Turks, and finding all roads closed to him, he turned south towards the Great Waste. A messenger from his father and from Mubarak found him. "We are anxious about you," they wrote, "and advise you to return to Kuwait. The time is not ripe for action."

In the palm-groves at Jabrin, Ibn Saud called his men together and put the facts before them ; he was himself determined to go on ; nothing would persuade him to give up even if he had to fight on alone ; with the help of God he would take what chances the desert brought to him ; those who wished might go.

Some went. There remained with him only stout-hearted, taciturn, grumpy Jiluwi, Mohamed his brother, the original thirty who set out with him from Kuwait, and ten new men from Riad. Some fifty in all with their slaves. These Ibn Saud bound by oath to stand by him to the end.

His position was precarious. He had set out with high hopes, believing that he had only to show himself and all Nejd would join him against the Rashid and that he would be leading an army. Yet he was no more than an outlaw: there were spies watching him and reporting on his moves, and scouts out in every direction to see which way he went; he was an outcast to all the tribes; the hand of every man in the desert was against him, for, in the desert, failure made an enemy of every man.

But he did not lose heart. He was always most dangerous when things went wrong. His belief in himself was as strong as ever.

"Go back," he said to the messenger, "go back and tell my father what you have seen and heard. Tell him that no more will I endure with patience that our country be under the heel of the Rashid and that our family be trodden in the dust. I will gamble success against death. I will not return until I have succeeded. Death is better than failure. All things are in the hands of God the Most Merciful."

CHAPTER XII

IBN SAUD considered carefully what next to do. He saw that this raiding was useless, especially with only a handful of men: it could effect no definite result. His one hope was to make a coup so dramatic as to startle. He decided to make a dash at Riad itself.

He sent one of his men to spy. The man reported that there was a strong Rashid garrison in the town which was holding the Almasmak fort and the principal points: the Governor, a Shammar sheik named Ajlan, lived in a house opposite the fort. The people of Riad and of all Nejd were dissatisfied; they hated the Rashid and prayed for a Saud to come back to rule them, but they would never rise by themselves. They must have a leader.

It was clear that with his few men Ibn Saud could not attack openly. His attack must be a surprise.

The first thing was to hide his intentions. He must disappear and lie low. Giving out word that all his men had deserted him, he made with them into the empty, peopleless country to the south.

For fifty days he made no raid nor showed himself; but it was a difficult time. His men, like all desert Arabs, were easily swayed by passing events. Success stimulated them to any heights and failure dragged them down to the depths. Inaction they could not stand. It needed all Ibn Saud's personality to keep them together. They had lived hard before, but with the excitement of loot and raiding to spur them on. Now they almost starved. For food they had a few dates rationed out and occasionally some meat when they shot a sand-deer. Water they got from the rare desert wells. They would creep up—taking all precautions that they were not seen—uncover a well, fill their skins, cover up their traces and creep away. The water they rationed carefully. By the time it was finished it was slimy and stank of the skins. Where they could find a little scrub for the camels they halted, sleeping in the open, but all the time they had to be on tiptoe, watching and scouting out to see that they were not observed, as the news would travel at once through the tribes.

As day passed day without action the men grew restless, muttered and argued. They wanted action or to get back to their women. A life without fighting or their women was not worth living. But Ibn Saud refused to let them go home even for a day or two: they might talk: they might never come back. He strove with them. With all his persuasive skill he argued with this one, threatened that one, appealed to the pride of another, and gripped them all so that he held them to the one purpose. He had the quality, rare among desert Arabs, of persistent, sustained, dogged effort. Nothing would turn him once he had made up his mind.

The strain was all the greater, for the Month of Fasting had begun. Ibn Saud, Jiluwi, and many of the men kept the Fast rigidly, neither eating nor drinking for an hour before the dawn until the sunset.

On the twentieth day of the Fast, after they had said the evening prayer and broken bread, Ibn Saud gave the order to move. They travelled cautiously, moving by night, avoiding any tracks or paths, and halting by day. The moon was in the last quarter, and the nights were black dark, so that they put out scouts well ahead to avoid stumbling into an encampment or across stray shepherds. They were forced to move slowly, for their camels were in a bad state, very lean and full of mange.

At the wells of Abu Jifan they kept the Festival of the Id, which ended the Fast, and then reached the foot of the Tuwaiq hills which run northwards close past Riad. Here Ibn Saud gave the order to move quickly : there were villages in the hollows : they might be seen : they must reach Riad before a warning could get ahead of them. They must force the camels to speed.

At the groves of Dil Alshuaib, which were an hour and a half by foot from Riad, he left the animals with twenty men and ordered them to join him only if he sent for them ; but that if they heard nothing within twenty-four hours they should take the road to Kuwait and tell his father that he was dead or a prisoner with the Rashid.

Now on foot he led the way through the palm-groves that stretched some miles to the south of the town. With him he had forty men. He had no clear plan of action. He had no confederates in the town. Trusting in God alone he would take what chance offered, seize any opportunity that came to him, and act as seemed good in the circumstances.

At Shamsieh, where the palm-groves ended and the gardens began, he halted. First he cut down a palm-tree, which with its rough bark made a passable ladder. Then picking out Jiluwi and six men, he left the rest under his brother Mohamed, with orders to keep in touch with those behind and to await his orders.

"Look you," he said, "if by to-morrow no message comes to you, haste away home also, for you will know that we are dead. There is no Power or Might save in God."

CHAPTER XIII

WITH Jiluwi and the six men behind him carrying the palm-trunk Ibn Saud crept forward through the gardens, by twisting paths, over mud walls, and across irrigation channels, listening for a watchman or a dog to give the alarm, until they came close under the town wall near by the great cemetery where the road to Mecca runs. Crouching in the dry moat, they listened. From far overhead they could hear the sentries in the fort. A watchman cried as he passed on his rounds and was gone. There was silence again. They had not been seen.

Putting the palm-trunk against the wall they swarmed up it one by one, keeping low, and dropped into the street beyond. It was mid-January. The night air was sharp. All the townspeople were indoors. Having muffled their arms in their clothes against noise, in single file they made down the empty streets to the house of Jowaisir the cowherd, which was close to that of the Governor.

Ibn Saud knocked. A woman cried out asking who was there.

"I am from the Governor," he replied, "come to see Jowaisir about buying two cows."

"Go away," called the woman, "do you think we are harlots? Go away. This is no time to come knocking on the door of a house where there are women."

"If you do not open," he answered, "I will tell the Governor, and to-morrow Jowaisir shall suffer." Then he stood aside and waited, with his men ready.

After a time a man looked out with the light of the room behind him. Two seized him so that he could not cry out, and all pressed into the house and closed the door. The man was an old servant from the palace.

"It is our master, Abdul Aziz," he cried as soon as he saw Ibn Saud, and all his family crowded in to do obeisance. He had the information they required.

The fort, he said, was full of Rashid soldiers. They took no special precautions and did not appear to expect an attack. The Governor usually went to the fort to sleep the night. A little after dawn his horses were brought for his inspection. After that he either went riding or walked over to his house. He never moved out without guards round him. His home was two doors off, and there were no sentries on it.

Reconnoitring stealthily, Ibn Saud and his men crept up and over the flat roof-tops. In the next house was a man and his wife asleep. Muffling them in their bedclothes they tied them up.

The Governor's house was next door and joined this house, but stood a story higher so that to get on to it they had to clamber up over each other's shoulders. Once up, they lay stretched out on the flat roof, listening. There was no sound of alarm. They had not been seen or heard.

Moving silently on bare feet down into the house, they found the servants in the basement and locked them together in a room under a guard. On the second floor they found the Governor's bedroom.

Ibn Saud slipped a cartridge into the breach of his rifle. Leaving his men at the door and with Jiluwi beside him carrying a lighted candle, which he shaded with one hand, he tiptoed across the room to the bed against the farther wall. There were two people in it, but they were both women. They were the Governor's wife and her sister.

The wife sat up in terror. Ibn Saud clapped a hand over her mouth while Jiluwi dealt with her sister.

The Governor's wife was a woman of Riad called Mutliba, whose father had worked in the palace for Abdur Rahman, so Ibn Saud knew her.

"Be quiet, Mutliba," he said, " or I will kill you. I see you have played the slut and married one of these Shammar swine."

" My lord," she replied, when he had released her, " I am no slut. I only married after you had left us. And for what do you come here ? "

" I have come to kill Ajlan."

"Ajlan is in the fort," she replied. "He has at least eighty men with him; so escape before he finds and kills you."

" When does he come back to the house ? " he asked.

" Not until the sun is an hour up the sky," she replied.

" Then keep quiet, for if you make a sound we will cut your throats," he said, and locked the two women in with the servants.

The night was now far spent and there were but four hours before the dawn. He reconnoitred to see what to do.

In the front of the house was a large room, and in the room an alcove with latticed windows. Below the windows was a square, and opposite, across the square, the fort with a big double and iron-studded door in a high wall. Above the wall a sentry paced. Ibn Saud decided to rush the Governor when he came out and burst into the fort in the confusion.

First, he sent off two men to fetch Mohamed and his party, and when they had come he set watchers by the windows, and with his men settled down to pass the hours that move on leaden feet before the dawn. Squatted round on the floor they listened to one who recited passages from the Koran. They prayed, each man to himself, sat in contemplation, and settled any quarrels there were between them. After that they slept a little.

When it grew towards morning the servant brought them coffee, bread and dates. After they had eaten they performed the morning prayer softly, drawn up in two lines across the room with Ibn Saud in front leading and did their obeisances towards Mecca. Then they looked to their arms and got ready for what the day should bring them.

CHAPTER XIV

A LITTLE after sunrise one of the watchers called. Ibn Saud crept to the window. Outside in the square some slaves were leading up the Governor's horses. In the fort there was movement.

Ibn Saud gave his final orders. Four men were to stay at the window and as soon as they saw him running across the square to open fire on the guards at the fort gate. The rest to follow him.

He watched while the double gates were thrown open, and the Governor, Ajlan, came out with his guards behind him and walked across to his horses.

Now was the time. With a call to his men, Ibn Saud ran down the stairs, out of the house into the square, and with a great shout raced straight at Ajlan, who whipped round, drew his sword and struck at him. Ibn Saud parried the blow with his rifle and grappled with Ajlan and both fell fighting to the ground.

The guard scattered and ran for the fort. One made a thrust at Ibn Saud and was cut down by Jiluwi. Ajlan fought back furiously. He struggled free and made a run for the fort gate, shouting the alarm. Ibn Saud snatched up his rifle and fired at him, wounded him in the arm so that he dropped his sword, dived at him, and caught him by the legs as he got to the gate and clung hold of a post. The sentries from inside rushed to the gate. Ibn Saud's men rushed up from the outside. On the steps they fought, a mob of men struggling, shouting, slashing at each other. From above on the wall and through the loopholes the garrison opened fire and hurled down blocks of stone.

A man next to Ibn Saud went down shot : another was wounded and lay writhing. Ajlan's guards grappled with Ibn Saud. Ajlan got one leg free and kicked back, hitting Ibn Saud a tremendous blow in the groin, which sent him reeling in pain. He let go of Ajlan and the guard dragged him through the gateway and tried to swing to the gate. Jiluwi with three men hurled himself on to the gate and heaved it open. Ajlan was running for the mosque across the fort courtyard. From all the walls the garrison was firing down. After Ajlan went Ibn Saud and Jiluwi, with their swords drawn, and Jiluwi cut him down on the steps of the mosque.

Then they made for the staircase. They were completely outnumbered. Two of Ibn Saud's men lay dead : four were seriously wounded. They were thirty against eighty, but they had the drive of victory behind them. Led by Ibn Saud and Jiluwi they stormed their way up to the parapets, killed or wounded half the garrison and threw their bodies down into the courtyard where they were dashed to pieces, and drove the rest into a room where they surrounded them.

At once Ibn Saud sent criers through the town, on to the mosques and the fort wall, to warn the people that he had captured the fort.

The population of Riad rose. They were tired of the Rashid and his injustices. They wiped out the other posts of Rashid soldiers in the town, and welcomed Ibn Saud with open arms. The remainder of the garrison in the fort surrendered. Ibn Saud was master of Riad.

PART III

CHAPTER XV

IBN SAUD had taken Riad, but he held little else. The villagers and tribesmen of Nejd still would not rise and join him. They had often before seen a town taken by a raid and lost within the same day. For twenty years the Sauds had been continually beaten by the Rashid. They waited cautiously. Only a few hundred hardy ones joined him. With these, his old companions, and the people of Riad he could not hope to stand up to the Rashid with his prestige and all his thousands of fighting men of the Shammar tribes behind him.

Riad he was determined to hold at all costs. He set to work to make it impregnable before the Rashid counter-attacked. The whole population turned out to help him. In many places the walls were broken. They built them up with feverish energy, expecting an attack at any moment. They re-dug the moat and built towers and loopholes for rifles. They brought in provisions and stored them, and unearthed rifles and ammunition which had been hidden during the rule of the Rashid. Ibn Saud worked out the details of the defence and organised the men into a garrison.

When the news of this came to the Rashid he sneered.

"The poor fool," he said, "he is as a bird that has flown into the snare." For the moment he was busy with other things. He considered Ibn Saud of no great importance. As soon as he was ready he would come down and teach this cheap, filibustering raider and the people of Riad a lesson : he would show them that they could not murder his Governor and flout him in this way.

Ibn Saud had no intention of being caught in any snare. He had no military training : he knew nothing of the maxims of

Napoleon, but he had an instinctive military sense which warned him not to get caught in the walled town by a superior force. Riad he would make able to stand a siege, but he himself would get out into the open country and keep his mobility of action.

He sent word of his success to his father begging him to come to Riad as he would trust the defence of the town to no one else.

Abdur Rahman slipped quietly away out of Kuwait with his son Abdullah, and taking the road into the Hasa made for Riad. He had to travel with caution, for the whole countryside was full of the Rashid's men, and the Rashid himself was advancing on Riad. Ibn Saud sent Jiluwi with 150 horsemen to meet him. By taking unfrequented tracks across the Dahna Desert, they came at last, after many difficulties, safe to Riad.

The people of Riad received Abdur Rahman as their ruler with acclaim. A few days later he summoned the ulema, the Doctors of the Law, and the notables and before them abdicated his rights and nominated Ibn Saud as his successor. He gave him as a symbol the sword of Saud the Great, which, for a hundred years, had been handed down by the Sauds from father to son. It was a fine sword, the blade of Damascus steel, the handle covered with gold, and the scabbard inlaid with silver.

Though a man of action and a fighter, even in his youth Abdur Rahman had been studious and devout. As he grew older he became more sedentary and even more religious. He spent long hours in reading the Koran and the Holy Writings. He shut himself away in contemplation. He was always ready to advise and encourage his sons, but he did not wish to lead them any more. It required a young man to lead in the fighting that was ahead.

Ibn Saud treated his father as before with great respect. At public prayers he stood behind him, letting the old man take the place of Imam. He deferred to him often, listened to his advice, but from now on Ibn Saud was the ruler of Riad and the claimant to rulership of Nejd and beyond that of all Arabia.

NOTE: *See Map on page 297 to illustrate Ibn Saud's conquest of Arabia.*

CHAPTER XVI

AS soon as Ibn Saud was satisfied that the town could stand a siege, he handed over the defence to his father and brothers. Taking a force of picked men with a hundred camels and forty horses, and his brother Sad, he set out. Sad was his favourite brother, much like himself in build and temperament. He was only a youth but he had the same great shoulders, the same genial manner, the same courage and love of a fight, and the same sudden bursts of fierce anger; but he had not Ibn Saud's judgment or self-control.

Keeping Riad as his base Ibn Saud made to the south, into the districts known as the Aflaj and the Harj, which formed the southern half of Nejd. Here the sheiks were of the Dawasir tribes and related to his mother, and the people were stout-hearted and had always been hostile to the Rashid.

He worked on a definite scheme. He went from village to village, rousing the people, organising their defences, giving them arms, and now and again putting in a few fighting men to encourage them.

The Rashid soldiers came after him, but they could never corner him. He never stopped to fight, but moved at a great speed. They found the whole countryside bit by bit prepared against them. If they went into a village they might be caught in an ambush. If they attacked the villagers would resist, and suddenly out of the blue would come Ibn Saud on their rear. He raided their camps at night. If a detachment were isolated he surrounded and wiped it out. They had successes, took a village, beat Ibn Saud off with loss, but always he came back, and the villagers and tribesmen were filled with a new spirit and fought them.

The fear of Ibn Saud grew on them. He came tearing down on them unexpectedly from all directions. He became a legend. His taking of Riad with six men was told all round the camp-fires and grew in the telling. He had throttled a man with one hand. The legend grew until he was a giant twice the size of ordinary men. He had taken on three men at once and split all their heads open with his sword. He had carried off a man in a fight, picking him up at full gallop, slinging him across the horse, and then let him go with a present as if he did it out of pure devilment. He covered distances with such speed that he appeared to be in two places at once.

The Rashid determined to be done with all this. Though a bad ruler, he was a good soldier. He realised that he had under-estimated Ibn Saud. Collecting a large force of Shammar tribesmen he came south from Hail to deal with him.

When he was near Riad his spies warned him that the town was now walled and garrisoned and ready to resist him: he would have to besiege it if he wished to take it. His advisers urged him to occupy the wells round the town and cut off the water-supply, but he did not want a siege: he wanted a dramatic capture when he could make an example of the rebels. He had heard that Ibn Saud had bolted south and was afraid to meet him. He would go after him. Dilam, the capital of the Harj, which lay south of Riad, had declared for Ibn Saud. He would feint at Riad, but pass it and make straight for Dilam.

His manœuvre succeeded. He reached the village of Najan, four miles to the north of Dilam, unnoticed, and rested for the night. He would march into Dilam by daylight in full state and make an example of the town.

CHAPTER XVII

IBN SAUD was far away down in the south. As soon as he heard of the Rashid's advance he realised that the crucial time was come. His taking of Riad was a quick raid, of no great permanent military value except that it had given him prestige. Now he must meet the Rashid in the open and fight him. He had sent out the reports of his own flight to draw the enemy as far south as possible.

He set to work to collect a force. His own men were a mere handful, good for a raid but useless for a battle. Day and night he travelled up and down the country, urging the headmen of the villages and the sheiks of the tribes to join him; but they lagged. They came only reluctantly. They were still afraid of the Rashid and his Shammar fighters. Gradually Ibn Saud drove out their fears and roused them to enthusiasm.

He worked continuously. He slept little. He ate sparingly and as he travelled. He covered great distances and spent all the hours of rest in earnest argument, more wearying than travelling, until even his constitution felt the strain. At last he had collected a thousand fighting men and given them a rendezvous at the village of Hauta, when late one afternoon a scout riding hard brought the news that the Rashid lay at Najan, ready to attack Dilam.

There was no time to lose. It was seventy miles from Hauta to Dilam. With all the men who had arrived he set off. He must get there before dawn. To mislead any spies he gave out that he was going westwards and rode north along the foot of the Tuwaiq hills.

He urged his men to hurry. His own riding camel was fast,

but she was tired so that in the dark she often stumbled on the rough ground and once, when he struck her with his riding cane, she fell and threw him. A bedouin riding close behind him tripped over him and came down with a crash with his camel on top of him. Behind came more men and camels. Out of the tumult, camels roaring and struggling, men shouting, confusion, his guards dragged Ibn Saud free. He was badly bruised and partly stunned.

As soon as he could sit up he climbed back into the saddle. He would not halt a minute. All that night he drove his men, whipping up the laggards, keeping the straggling column of camel and horsemen together, urging them forward. He was in great pain, but refused to give in and allowed neither his men nor himself any rest, so that they reached Dilam while it was still dark.

To the north of the town towards Najan was a belt of palmtrees. In these Ibn Saud distributed his force. Entering the town with his guards he ordered the gates to be closed and the walls to be manned.

Then he collapsed. He was worn out. For seven days he had been continuously on the move without sleep and with only a handful of dates for food. His guards carried him into a house, rubbed him with oil and wrapped him in blankets, and he şlept until the call to the midday prayer. Then he woke, stiff and sore from his fall, but refreshed and ready.

CHAPTER XVIII

MEANWHILE as soon as it was day, the Rashid advanced with a screen of mounted scouts ahead of his main body. As they came to the palm-groves Ibn Saud opened fire on them: four horses and six men were killed, and the rest galloped back.

The Rashid sent more men ahead, but when these were held up he realised that he had in front of him, not the townsfolk of Dilam but some regular fighting men. All that day and the next morning he tried to find out their numbers and dispositions by raids and small attacks, but Ibn Saud held his men in. He had allotted places in the line for the coming fight to each tribe, and given them orders to keep concealed, using only the minimum force to hold off the enemy's raids; and so to mislead the Rashid into thinking that he had only a few men in front of him.

He had just returned to Dilam and was sitting down to the midday meal when the alarm was sounded. The enemy were advancing across the open in a long double line. The Rashid, piqued at the holding up of his plans, had determined to walk through the resistance and brush it aside. He marched with his banners flying, his footmen in the centre, and on the flanks his cavalry brandishing their swords and shouting.

Still Ibn Saud held his fire. It was not easy, for his men were wild with excitement at the coming fight, straining to be let go. When the enemy were close he gave the order. The sudden burst of rifle-fire staggered and broke their lines. They had expected a few stray shots and not a solid hail of bullets. They hesitated. At once with his men behind him, yelling his battle-cry, Ibn Saud rode straight at them. They gave back. They started to run. The run became a panic. After them at full gallop came Ibn Saud with his tribesmen and the people of Dilam. They smashed into the running enemy, broke them up, and drove them over the plains in full retreat with the Rashid leading the way, up past Riad and beyond until the pursuit was stopped only by lack of ammunition and the weariness of the animals.

The news went out like a flash. It was a victory: the first time for many years that a Saud had beaten the Rashid. All the Harj and the Aflaj rose, drove out the remainder of the Rashid's men and joined Ibn Saud. All southern Nejd was with him.

But the Rashid had a stout heart. He was not finished so easily. He realised that he must fight for his life, and without delay, before Ibn Saud grew any stronger. As soon as he reached Hail he collected a new force and feinted at Kuwait. Mubarak called to Ibn Saud for help. Ibn Saud marched out of Riad eastwards towards Kuwait.

This was what the Rashid wanted. Having drawn his enemy away he turned south and made a rush at Riad, but Abdur Rahman was ready for him and held him off from the walls.

As soon as the news reached Ibn Saud he did not hurry back to Riad, but cut westward across the enemy's line of retreat and harried his villages. The Shammar, afraid for their homes and families, broke up, scattered and made homewards as fast as they could. The Rashid's army had disappeared.

Taking his chance, Ibn Saud took village after village and threw out the Rashid's men from Shagra, Thamida, and Thadiq, until he controlled the country of Nejd for fifty miles north of Riad.

CHAPTER XIX

THESE successes gave Ibn Saud a new position. He held half Nejd. He had made a name for himself as a fighter. He had driven the Rashid almost back on to his own ground. He had a considerable force, more men were coming in daily, and he could fight the Rashid in the open.

Backwards and forwards they fought all that autumn of 1902 and the spring of 1903 until a great drought and famine in that year held them up. Bit by bit Ibn Saud established himself.

It was a personal duel between Ibn Saud and the Rashid. The Rashid could count on his Shammar tribes round Hail. Ibn Saud could count on the people of Riad and the surrounding districts. These formed a nucleus. Beyond these their forces were constantly changing. Other tribes joined them, the Mutair, the Harb, the Ataiba, the Ajman, but they had no loyalty to one or the other. They were fickle and treacherous. They would change sides in a night. The pique or ambition of a sheik, the promise of gold or loot, a small defeat would set them attacking their own allies or raiding them as they retreated. There was no regular army on either side. The personalities of the leaders were the decisive factors.

The Rashid was short, dark, lowering in looks, brusque in manner; a harsh, unlovable man and ungenerous. He had no patience and no ability to handle the tribesmen. He understood force only. He ruled by force. He fought for loot. He was a freebooter and a destroyer.

Ibn Saud was open-handed and large-hearted. He had unlimited patience. He knew how to deal with the tribesmen, how to flatter their pride and how to ignore their follies. He had the characteristics which the Arabs admire : he was generous and liberal : he was a great lover, a brave and skilful fighter, and, despite his Wahabi upbringing, he enjoyed laughter and boasting. Moreover, he had youth and faith. The Rashid was getting old and casual. Ibn Saud believed in himself. He believed in his people and that once again he would make them great. He could inspire his men with his own inspiration. He conquered not to destroy but to rule, and as he advanced he did not loot but consolidated what he had taken by promises of prosperity.

Late in 1903, when the first rain had come and the famine had broken and there was grazing to be found and water in the wells, Ibn Saud advanced northwards. Between him and the country of the Shammar was the Qasim, the richest district of old Nejd, of which Anaiza and Buraida were the principal towns. The Rashid still held the district, but the people were for Ibn Saud.

He swept quickly over the Qasim, meeting with little resistance —for the Rashid was far away in the north dealing with a revolt of his own tribesmen—defeated and killed Husein Jarrid the Rashid Governor of the district, took Anaiza, and surrounded and besieged Buraida, which was strongly fortified and garrisoned and had shut its gates against him.

Collecting such men as he could the Rashid sent them under Obaid one of his cousins to the relief of his garrison in Buraida.

Ibn Saud turned on Obaid and beat him back in a fierce fight. The Shammar tribesmen broke and ran for home. Obaid was captured.

Ibn Saud was seated on his Arab mare when Obaid was brought before him.

" So," he said, looking down at him, " it is Obaid ibn Rashid, he who murdered my uncle Mohamed in Riad."

Dismounting he drew his sword, which his father had given him and which now he carried always. For a while he balanced the sword in his hand.

" Do not kill me, O Abu Turki," cried Obaid.

" This is no place for mercy," replied Ibn Saud. " I will do justice, the justice of just revenge for murder."

He struck three times, deftly with the wrist and forearm. With the first blow he struck low to hamstring, and as Obaid swayed to the blow he struck higher cutting deep into his neck so that the blood spurted out as from a broken pipe, and with the third, quick and supple as a whip lash, while the man sagged but before he fell, he cut him open so that his heart lay exposed as it beat and shivered and palpitated.

Then he kissed the sword, drew the blade clean and sheathed it.

The garrison in Buraida, now without hope of relief, surrendered, and all the Qasim up to the country of the Shammar accepted Ibn Saud. He had forced the Rashid out of Nejd. Nejd was once more under a Saud.

When Ibn Saud marched back to Riad even the most sour-faced Wahabis came out to meet him with joy. In the Great Mosque, with the consent of the Elders, the religious leaders, the governors, and the sheiks, after the midday prayer he was solemnly declared by his father to be Amir of all Nejd and Imam of the Wahabis.

PART IV

CHAPTER XX

THE rapid success of Ibn Saud did not, however, suit the Turks. As before they were the nominal rulers of all Arabia, but they held only its fringes with troops and their governors, in the Yemen, up the Red Sea Coast through the Hejaz, across Syria and down the Euphrates river to Baghdad; and along the Persian Gulf to the Hasa—a ring of rich lands round the Inner Desert. And as ever they played the tribes one against the other, backing the weak against the strong. They had opposed the Rashid when he was strong. Now they opposed Ibn Saud.

Lately old Abdul Hamid, the Turkish Sultan, had been fired with ambition: to revive the Ottoman Empire; to become a great Sultan and Caliph as his ancestors had been before him; and to rule in Central Arabia itself.

The Germans encouraged him. They had already started building the Baghdad railway towards the east, and were sending out traders and agents into the Persian Gulf, and watching for the chance to outwit the English, to push them out of the Gulf and to take Kuwait.

For them Ibn Saud was dangerous. He was in alliance with Mubarak of Kuwait. He was said to be friendly with the English. He was farther away and more difficult to control than the Rashid. They encouraged Abdul Hamid to use the Rashid.

Abdul Hamid sent more troops to the Yemen and the Hejaz, increased the garrisons in Baghdad and the Hasa, ordered a railway to be built from Damascus down the Hejaz to Medina, and made an agreement with the Rashid that he should rule

Central Arabia as his representative. Ibn Saud was interfering with his plans. The Rashid, his nominee, was calling for help. He ordered the Governor of Baghdad to send troops to smash Ibn Saud.

Early in the summer of 1904, eight battalions of regular Turkish troops with six light guns slung between mules marched out of Samarah, a village on the Euphrates river, to the rendezvous to which the Rashid had called the Shammar tribes, and with them advanced into Nejd and threatened Anaiza and Buraida.

Ibn Saud collected every man he could to meet them. Finding them entrenched in a camp near the village of Bukariya he camped over against them.

The Rashid was well supplied. Besides arms and men the Turks had sent him money. Ibn Saud was short of all supplies. He had not enough rations for his men. That night they must sleep hungry. Except for a handful of dates they had nothing to eat all day. They were grumbling and disheartened. It was a poor preparation for a fight, but he could only promise them food when they took the enemy's camp.

Towards evening he went out to reconnoitre the ground ahead, when he saw away to the east a cloud of dust up against the evening sun. More men for the Rashid, he concluded, but his scouts reported that it was not fighting men but a small raiding party bringing sheep into the enemy's camp.

At once Ibn Saud called his men to horse. There was no time to saddle or bridle. Leading the way he galloped them close past the Shammar camp, straight for the sheep, cut down the escort, and each man heaved a sheep up over his horse's cruppers and turned for home.

Already the Shammar were out after them, far outnumbering them, firing from the saddle and shouting as they came.

Ibn Saud with a few men dashed across their front to head them off. After him they went, realised their mistake and turned back too late to cut off the rest. It was a running fight at full gallop in the gloaming.

That night Ibn Saud's camp was full of life; the raid had excited and put new life into the men. They were boasting of the exploits of Ibn Saud and what they would do with the Shammar on the morrow. They ate meat and were satisfied.

Before dawn Ibn Saud attacked—it was July 15th, and the heat was intense.

He sent his men at the enemy's flanks. Time and again they drove the Shammar tribesmen back, but always the Turkish infantry stood firm in the centre and the tribesmen rallied round them.

In the late forenoon the Turks opened with their guns. Ibn Saud's men were not used to shells and began to give. He rode ahead, exposing himself to encourage them. A shell burst close beside him; a splinter took away half a finger of his left hand and the shrapnel wounded him in the left knee. Streaming with blood he was forced to draw off. His men began to panic and run. With difficulty he held them together, gave them heart and retired back in some formation.

The Rashid was too badly mauled to come after him. He had lost a thousand men. The Turks could do nothing in the great heat. They made camp outside the village of Shinanah, let Ibn Saud go, and turned instead to subdue the villages of the Qasim and northern Nejd.

CHAPTER XXI

NEVER did Ibn Saud show himself better than in defeat. When things were bad and everyone round him in despair he grew genial and optimistic.

His wounds, which would have incapacitated an ordinary man, hardly held him up. He had them bandaged and laughed at them. He set to work at once. He had to find allies and make a confederacy.

He sent out messengers to the Mutair, the Ataiba and the Dawasir and even far away to the north to the tribes of the Muntafik and the Anazah.

With infinite patience he dealt personally with the quarrelsome, touchy sheiks. It needed rare skill and tact to persuade them to settle their differences, smooth over their feuds, and combine to one object. It was as if one collected the thousand jagged pieces of a broken vase, and joined the pieces together, knowing that one mistake, one blow, would smash it again into a thousand jagged pieces. He argued that they must all fight the Rashid, for he had brought in the Turks, and that if the Turks came with the Germans behind them it would be the end of their freedom.

Hobbling from his knee-wound he went among his own people, rousing them, cheering them, collecting every man with a rifle, and before the Rashid and the Turks realised it, he was at them with a new force.

He found them marching up the dry bed of the Rima river. They were coming back to the camp at Shinanah after subduing some of the Nejd villages. Before they could form to meet him Ibn Saud attacked.

Again his men drove the Shammar back on the flanks and, again the Turkish regular troops stood firm as a rallying point, but the Mutair who were on Ibn Saud's left wing began to give. He realised that if he was defeated a second time he was done. Collecting all the men he could, leading the way with his bodyguard behind him and shouting the name of his sister Nura as his war-cry he charged on horseback straight at the Turkish centre.

The Turkish line bent and broke. Ibn Saud burst through them and then back again, cutting them down. The Shammar seeing the Turks break scattered and ran.

The Turks re-formed. Ibn Saud surrounded them. That night they started to retreat in formation. The next day they plodded on across the sand.

They were parched by the blistering sun. They ran out of water. They lost their way. They were in thick uniforms and heavily laden, a desperate column of weary men plodding forward with their heads down.

Round them Ibn Saud sent his light-moving Arabs, swarming like flies, harrying them with incessant raids and sniping. Some fell out and the bedouin women cut their throats. Some straggled and were cut down by the horsemen. Some surrendered and a few limped painfully back to Basra.

CHAPTER XXII

THE Turks could not allow such a defeat to go unrevenged. It struck at the basis of their prestige in Arabia. They began to prepare a large force on the Euphrates to deal with Ibn Saud decisively.

Those round Ibn Saud, his advisers and the Wahabi leaders were arrogant with success, full of boasting and war talk, but he had no delusions. He saw clearly that, though he had defeated the Turkish nominee, the Rashid, and the few Turks with him, yet if the Turkish Empire put out its strength it could crush him. He must avoid that. He would go slowly and fobb the danger off while it was still far away. He got into touch with Muklis Pasha, the Governor of Basra, and persuaded Mubarak to act as intermediary.

Mubarak arranged a meeting at which Abdur Rahman on behalf of Ibn Saud and Muklis Pasha met and came to terms: the Turks recognised Ibn Saud as the ruler of Nejd including the Qasim on condition that they kept a nominal force in the district and garrisons in Anaiza and Buraida.

The danger of serious attack was for the moment postponed.

The Turkish garrisons arrived but very soon found themselves isolated. Ibn Saud gave them no help. They could not keep order or security. All the roads became infested with raiders who looted the convoys which brought their ammunition and supplies from Basra. They could do nothing in retaliation. If they moved outside the walls of the towns in small numbers, they were surrounded and killed. If they went out in large numbers they moved too slowly to catch the light-moving bedouin.

At the end of a year the Turkish soldiers were in rags, almost reduced to starvation. In some places they were eating the pith of the date-palms for their only ration. Many were selling their arms for a little food. They had nicknamed the Qasim "The Devil's Daughter." They were without heart or spirit. Dying of disease and the violence of the sun they were deserting in numbers.

The Turkish Government pressed Ibn Saud to give them active help. He gave them fair words but no help. They tried him with a subsidy in gold. He needed gold. It was the handle to all power. It meant arms and allies. He needed it urgently, but with a gesture he refused and returned a present the Turks had sent him.

He had in fact realised that conditions had changed. The Turks were in difficulties. The Yemen and the Hejaz were in revolt. Syria was honeycombed with revolutionary committees, working for Arab independence and to eject the Turks. In the Balkans, in Egypt, in Turkey, and in Constantinople itself there were disorder and the threat of upheaval and revolution.

He knew that now the Turks could not concentrate against him nor even supply or help their garrisons in the Qasim. He might have attacked them, defeated them, and driven them out by force and so gained renown and prestige. Those round him urged him to take action. He preferred to wait and to let time and necessity work for him.

As he had foreseen, needing every man they could mobilise and realising their helplessness, the Turks reduced their garrisons in the Qasim and then withdrew them. They had learned their lesson. Leaving a few garrisons along the Hasa coast they went and returned no more to Central Arabia.

CHAPTER XXIII

HAVING jockeyed the Turks into going without making war, Ibn Saud was once more face to face with his rival the Rashid.

He was on the top of the tide now, winning. His renown was growing. More and more tribesmen were joining him, but he could not relax.

Rashid was as stout-hearted as himself. The desert was full of chances. One serious error and his fickle, treacherous allies would leave him and his patchwork of alliances would tear to pieces under him.

During these years he lived in constant danger. He must be always ready not only for the enemy's raids and sudden night attacks, but also for treachery in his own camp. Any night his closest allies might turn on him and murder him.

His tent was always pitched either clear of the camp or so that there were no other tents before or behind it; his bodyguard close round him. He slept but little, some two or three hours a night.

When on active service he never used a bed but lay on a rug on the sand with his drawn sword beside him. Sometimes he did not even lie down but squatted on his heels, his chin on his hands and his hands folded over the hilt of his sword stuck upright in the sand.

From sleep he could, like a coiled snake, in one movement come straight into the striking position.

Once a servant blundered into his tent without warning and Ibn Saud had sliced his shoulder and arm away before the man could call out. His horse stood picketed by the tent, and if there were an alarm he was up and away riding without saddle or bridle.

He became as lean and muscular as a wild animal. The desert life kept his body taut and as firm as marble. He had no liking for sedentary town life. He ate and drank sparingly. His vigour was immense. He worked all day and most of the night. He would sit in the mouth of his tent interviewing all who came, hearing complaints, deciding cases, listening to reports, and judging the truth of the news. He had a great knowledge of the country and the lives and histories of all the tribes. He saw personally to details of camp and food arrangements and gave his own orders and made the plans of action. Even when he was busiest he performed his religious observances strictly, fasted, read the Koran, and prayed five times a day.

When there was a raid or a fight he was the first on the move, eyes afire and as excited as a boy going out to play.

Except for his very few hours of sleep he was never still. He wore out those round him and he fought the Rashid steadily back until at last he cornered and finished him.

The Rashid had been raiding. After a long march he came to the village of Muhanna and camped. His men were tired. He himself was growing more and more disheartened and casual as he grew older. Believing that Ibn Saud was many miles away he took no special precaution for the night.

Ibn Saud was in fact many miles away, but as soon as his scouts brought him the news he made a forced march in the dark. At dawn a thick dust storm blew up. Under cover of this he attacked, caught the enemy unprepared, and smashed them into flight.

The Rashid could have escaped, but he stood his ground, shouting his battle-cry to rally his men. Almost alone he was shot down at close quarters. His head was stuck on a pole and paraded through the villages so that the tribes should know he was dead.

At once among the Shammar and in the Hail there was confusion. The Rashid's successor was a weakling. All the males of the family fought between themselves for power, killing and murdering each other. The tribes, without a strong man to lead them, dispersed to their homes to quarrel and fight among themselves.

They would have combined against an invader, but they had no desire to go conquering. For the time being they were no more danger to Ibn Saud.

PART V

CHAPTER XXIV

IBN SAUD was twenty-seven, enormous in build, strong, lean, and hard, an accepted leader with a reputation as a fierce fighter and all the prestige of victory behind him, a tremendous virile force of a man who had defeated the Turks, overthrown the Rashid, and conquered Nejd by the strength of his his own right arm.

But he was by no means established. Difficulties and dangers came crowding in on him from inside as well as from out. The desert Arabs would not accept a new master so easily. They were like sand, each tribe and individual a fiercely independent unit. Like sand they could be held together between strong hands, but they could not be moulded into one plastic piece. And if the strong hands grew slack or loosened, like sand they escaped and fell strewn out into units as fiercely independent as before.

They had joined Ibn Saud not out of loyalty but because they thought they would have more liberty to raid and loot, when the Rashid was beaten. But the hand of Ibn Saud was heavy on them. He forbade them to raid without his permission and he punished, without pity, all who disobeyed him. The tribesmen grew restless and rebellious under the restraint.

In Riad itself the ulema looked at Ibn Saud sideways. He was devout it was true. He prayed, fasted, and gave alms as should every good Moslem. He neither drank wine nor smoked nor used unseemly oaths. His private life was ordered in accordance with Islam and the conventions. As a strong, virile man he delighted in many wives, but he had no concubines, no stealthy liaisons or mistresses. No man could throw stones at him in this matter.

Nevertheless the Wahabi Elders were distrustful of him; he was too genial for their way of thinking; he was often gay and even laughed, which was indecorous behaviour to their sour minds: he was known to have allowed his fighting men to sing on the march; he had found that the people of Anaiza smoked tobacco openly, and he had not punished them. He had been a friend of Mubarak who, as all the world knew, was very irregular in his ways: he had hobnobbed with foreigners and even encouraged them to visit him.

For help Ibn Saud turned to his father. Abdul Rahman had a great reputation for sanctity and the Wahabis trusted him. They would listen to him when they would listen to no one else.

Nevertheless Ibn Saud had to walk delicately. The Elders watched him. They considered themselves as the keepers of the conscience of every man, as did in fact every Wahabi whether elder or simple worshipper—and especially as keepers of the conscience of the ruler of Riad. They criticised and checked him. They would have raised the country against him if they had proved him unorthodox.

Naturally hot tempered Ibn Saud was irritated by their interference and their acid criticisms, but he held himself in, hid his thoughts, and forebore with them.

From outside came greater dangers. Ibn Saud's success suited Mubarak no more than it suited the Turks. His policy was the same as that of the Turks. He wished always to protect Kuwait by creating a balance of power among the tribes in Central Arabia. Ibn Saud had upset that balance. He had become too strong and a threat to Kuwait itself.

Moreover, between Mubarak and Ibn Saud had arisen much ill-feeling. While Ibn Saud had been a penniless refugee Mubarak had treated him kindly. He continued to treat him as a refugee.

He gave him advice and expected him to follow it without question.

But Ibn Saud refused; he was no more a youth to be instructed; he was master of Nejd and a person of importance. He resented Mubarak's attitude of patronage and control. He was irritated at Mubarak's tone, and Mubarak was jealous of the success and the independence of his protégé. They met and corresponded with all due politeness, but Mubarak began to work against Ibn Saud and to make alliances to counterbalance him. He came quickly to an agreement with the Turks who gave him money.

Between Kuwait and Nejd lived the Mutair tribes. They were surly and ill-natured. They resented all control, and Ibn Saud had already claimed the right to rule over them. Mubarak bought over Feisal al Dawish their sheik, an uncompromising, salt-pickled warrior. He persuaded the Rashid family to end their quarrels and to join with the Mutair. Finally he persuaded the Governor of the town of Buraida to refuse to recognise Ibn Saud. He himself stood in the background and did not appear openly, but Ibn Saud knew that he was the master-mind behind the confederacy.

As soon as Ibn Saud heard that the Governor of Buraida had shut the gates against him, he marched out. He found a force of Shammar tribesmen between him and the town and attacked at once. During the fight his horse slipped. He was thrown and broke a collar-bone. At sunset both sides drew off without either having gained the superiority.

All that night Ibn Saud lay in agony in his tent on the sand. He twisted and turned and sweated with the pain of his shoulder, but he refused to give in. His men had lost heart when they had seen that he was hurt. Unless he lead them personally they would break and run.

At dawn he led them out and by midday he had driven the

Shammar back. Then he turned on the Mutair, beat them, and chased them into their own country.

He decided to make an example of them. The Mutair had changed their allegiance so often. They had submitted to him before and then joined his enemies. They were traitors. He had shown before that he could hold his hand and be patient. Now he would show them that he could use force.

He lashed out at the Mutair without mercy. He raided them, looted and burned their villages right up to the frontier of Kuwait. He hung their headmen and drove out Sheik Dawish. Having made up his mind that it was necessary, Ibn Saud was utterly ruthless. He branded his mark on the Mutair so that all the tribes should see what he had done and be afraid. He harried them relentlessly—" I draw the sword in the face of the bedouin," he said. " It is the argument they understand "—until they crawled to him and submitted.

Finally he turned on Buraida. The Governor he had appointed himself. The gates were still closed against him and the town prepared for a siege, but there were some of his men in the town who at the hour of evening prayer, when the garrison was in the mosque, opened the gates to Ibn Saud. The Governor brought to him fell on his knees. He expected that Ibn Saud would have him executed at once; but with a sneer Ibn Saud told him to stand up and then to take his family and be gone out of Nejd.

But he was determined that there should be no more trouble in Buraida. The town was strongly fortified. Its people were well known for their ill-natured malevolence. It was the key point of northern Nejd and the centre of all its trade. It had always been rebellious. He made his cousin Jiluwi the Governor.

Already Jiluwi was feared far and wide. From the taciturn youth who had helped Ibn Saud to raid Riad he had grown into a short thick-set man with stern features and great bodily strength, a renowned rider and judge of horses and camels, very silent, quick in decision, and ruthless in action. He was utterly loyal to Ibn

Saud. He had no personal ambition, but he was rigidly conscientious. He carried out the law to the letter. His judgments were swift and terrible. He kept rigid discipline among his people. While Ibn Saud was feared, Jiluwi instilled into all he ruled such terror that his word was law even to the most distant bedouin; and from the date that he became Governor of Buraida there was no more trouble in Northern Nejd.

CHAPTER XXV

HARDLY had Ibn Saud returned to Riad before new troubles were on him. In the previous year old Sultan Abdul Hamid had been deposed by the Committee of Union and Progress, a group of young revolutionaries in Constantinople.

The Committee, however, had retained the Sultan's policy of reviving the Empire; and being young and enthusiastic they had put more energy and vigour into it.

They determined to tighten up the control of the Central Government over the provinces of the Empire and to take a firmer grip of the Arab countries, especially Syria and those along the Red Sea Coast—the Hejaz with the sacred cities of Mecca and Medina, and the Yemen and the Asir farther to the south because they were rich.

They hurried forward the building of the railway from Damascus to Medina for this could transport soldiers as well as pilgrims, and they appointed one Husein ibn Ali as the Grand Sherif of Mecca and their Governor of the Hejaz.

Husein was a typical Arab-Turkish official, of which there were many in Constantinople. He had spent many years in the city, where his sons were brought up. He had held many official posts and was a Councillor of the Empire. In looks and manner he might have been a Turkish Pasha of the Sultan's court, a dignified old man already over fifty with a short well-kept beard, slow and pompous in speech using long and antiquated words for preference, conservative and religious, subtle in all the guiles of Turkish procrastination, very courteous yet obstinate, autocratic and suspicious. He had been chosen because he was of the Hashimite family of Mecca, and so a descendent of the Prophet Mohamed; and because the Turks trusted him to act as their faithful agent.

Almost at once Husein and Ibn Saud quarrelled. Between Nejd and the Hejaz lay a broad steppe of highlands where the tribes of the Ataiba grazed their flocks of sheep and camels. Through this country ran the caravan routes from Nejd into the Hejaz and to Mecca, and it was the key to the Hejaz and to the Red Sea Coast.

Over the Ataiba Ibn Saud claimed suzerainty with the right to call on them for fighting men and to levy his taxes. Husein refused to allow such a claim. He maintained that they were his subjects. Ibn Saud marched on to the Ataiba from the east and received their submission. Husein sent his son Abdullah, a fat week-kneed youth with a mouth full of boastings, to raid from the west. Ibn Saud marched farther and sent out his brother Sad to raid even wider. Husein himself was in the south, in the Yemen, helping the Turks to crush a revolt. As soon as the revolt was crushed he made a march to demonstrate his victory, back through the Ataiba, and forced them to submit. By chance his men surrounded and captured Sad.

Ibn Saud prepared to attack Husein, when from behind came a new danger. His cousins, the sons of his uncle Saud who had chased him out of the Hasa when he was a refugee and who still claimed that they were the heirs to Riad and Nejd, had raised the Ajman and marched into southern Nejd and threatened Riad. The Hazazina headmen of the town of Laila and all the disgruntled tribes had joined them.

Ibn Saud faced the facts. For him facts were far more important than pride. He was never foolhardy. He never battered his head against the wall of the impossible. He realised that, with this revolt behind him, he could not stand up to Husein. He wanted to get his brother back. As quickly as possible he came to terms with Husein; he made a " little peace " as he called it to tide over the crisis. In return for Sad he paid an indemnity and withdrew.

Then he acted like lightning. The revolt was close to Riad. It was a blow to the heart. It threatened his personal prestige. If he was defeated, even if he hesitated, compromised, or delayed he was done. He hit hard at once. He found his cousins at the village of Hariq, dashed at them, caught them unprepared, and smashed them.

The Ajman bolted back across the border into the Hasa. His cousins fled, some to the Hasa and some to take refuge with Husein of Mecca. The Hazazina and their local supporters made for Laila where Ibn Saud surrounded them.

He made up his mind that here in the south he must, as he had in the north, make an example. They, like the Mutair, were his subjects and now traitors. Systematically and without pity he harried their land. He sent his men to kill and loot in the villages round Qutain and Hauta and then to raze them to the ground. He turned on Laila, forced it to surrender without terms and condemned to death nineteen of the headmen and the Hazazina leaders.

He gave the condemned men twenty-four hours' grace. He sent messengers out through the country-side to summon the people. Before the main gate of the town he ordered a platform to be built. On this at dawn he took his seat with his sheiks and his bodyguard round him. Before the townsmen, villagers, and bedouin from far and near were formed into three sides of a huge square, where his Wahabi fighting-men kept order. Above them sat Ibn Saud, fierce in his anger, dominating and terrifying. The fate of every man there was in his hands.

He gave all the orders himself personally. From the town the nineteen condemned were marched out. In pairs they were led up and made to kneel at the foot of the platform. "There is no Might nor Power save in God," said Ibn Saud and made a sign at which a huge nego slave without his cloak and with a drawn sword in his hand stepped forward with his assistants behind him.

They carried out all the formalities of the state execution deliberately and with dignity, no savage pleasure in killing, but cold justice. The executioner with the point of his sword pricked each man as he came to him in the neck, and as the wretch stretched his neck stiff at the terror of the steel, with a back-hand blow he sliced through the neck. When eighteen were dead and the nineteenth knelt ready Ibn Saud pardoned him and bade him go free to tell what he had seen of the just vengeance of Ibn Saud.

After that he rose and spoke to the people, his voice rising in a great roar, telling them of the sin of rebellion and its punishment. Then he called to them to come nearer, dropped his voice and spoke to them as his well-beloved subjects. He bade them go and choose one who should act as their Governor, faithful to him; and he promised them that if they remained loyal they should rule themselves in peace.

Only, all that day the eighteen dead men lay strewn out on the sand, a massed horror in the clean sunlight, a feast for the flies, and a warning to rebels. After the sunset prayer they were buried with the due ceremonies.

The story of Laila was told from village to village and from camp-fire to camp-fire and grew in the telling. The fierce punishment ruthless, just, and without malice, and the unreasoning generosity caught the imagination of the Arabs. This was a man, they said, a man to rule them, a fierce fighting man, a just judge who knew his own mind and acted without hesitation or doubt, a man to be feared and obeyed.

The most distant tribesmen heard it and were afraid. They understood strength and justice. Ibn Saud gave them both. He was fit to be master and to rule them.

CHAPTER XXVI

AT last Ibn Saud had a breathing space in which he might organise and consolidate his position. He had ejected and killed the Rashid; the family split by quarrels could do nothing against him, and the Shammar tribes had no leader. He had crushed all internal revolts. He had driven out the Turks. In the spring of 1913 he went into the south country. All administration and all justice was in his hands, and there were many disputes and cases to be settled. Also he had determined to teach the bedouin that he was master and that without his permission he would allow no raiding.

The bedouin looked on raiding as their right from time immemorial. It was, after their women, their one great pleasure. Like some game it was regulated by codes and conventions evolved through the centuries so that in a raid there was much dust and noise, some good galloping and sword-play, some loot for the winners, but few wounds or hurts.

It meant, however, general insecurity. All the roads were unsafe. The caravans were looted. The merchants were forced to pay tribute to the tribal sheiks and even then they were plundered. The villagers lived in constant fear of attack.

Ibn Saud decided that he would break down the ancient customs. Tribute was his prerogative alone. The road should be safe, and the villagers live in peace under him. He had already forbidden all raiding. His orders had been ignored. News had come in that a clan of the Murra had attacked a caravan that was travelling under his special protection. He would teach the bedouin a lesson.

He swooped down on this Murra clan without warning. He wiped them out, leaving only a black smear of tents and bodies on the sand as a warning.

CHAPTER XXVII

IT was his custom to do all work in public. When he was in Riad he sat on the steps of the palace facing the great courtyard. On the march he sat in the mouth of his tent and in villages when it was most convenient in the open square, usually on the steps of the mosque. Round him were the local sheiks and headmen and his bodyguard, huge men specially picked from the Wahabis fighting men, and his negro slaves, dressed in long cloaks, all armed, a few with heavy sticks in their hands, and with them the executioners.

All manner of cases came before him, quarrels over wells or rights of pasturage, disputes over land boundaries, irrigation channels, ownership of camels; claims for looting, theft, damage or injury done in a fight or brawl, complaints of every description. Everyman had the right to come direct before him, without interference or application to a subordinate, either with a complaint or an appeal. Sometimes he would be lenient and generous. At other times he was stern and easily angered by a chance word or by opposition; and within the Law of the Koran, which lay down the penalties for crimes, he held the power of life and death, of immediate mutilation, flogging and fine.

He dealt with each case himself face to face with accuser and the accused. There were no lawyers or advocates to complicate the issue or to prove black to be white. He heard the evidence quickly and gave his decision from which there was no appeal.

A bedouin was accused of theft; the accusers stood forward and swore; the man had found a saddle-bag beside a dead camel and taken the saddle-bag. The evidence was good. Ibn Saud pronounced his verdict. The executioner led the man to the centre of the square and struck off his right hand, dipped it in hot oil to stop the bleeding and holding the arm aloft paraded him so that all might see the freshly hacked stump.

A woman and a man were accused of loose living. The woman was no more than a harlot. The man had brought in strong drink from Kuwait. Ibn Saud ordered her to be whipped out of the town by his guards and the man to be flogged before him at once, and, if he lived after that, to be expelled into the Hasa.

There had been a quarrel; a man had been killed; the murderer stood condemned to death. The dead man's relations compromised for a fine and Ibn Saud assessed the blood-money and let the man go.

A woman came crying that her neighbour's cow had broken into her garden that morning and eaten all her clover. Her neighbours denied it on oath. Ibn Saud bade the butcher kill and split open the cow; its stomach was full of clover. The carcase stayed with its owner, but he paid an indemnity for the clover and a heavy fine for his false oath.

All the time Ibn Saud was himself on trial. Round him whether it was in the square of a town or out in the desert, squatted many men listening and watching him, sizing him up, judging his value. He must be quick, just, and severe. He could not hide himself behind some Government machine or a privileged position and so create an illusion of wisdom. He was himself the government and the judge. If he hesitated, showed ignorance of the law or the customs, weakness, or lacked in judgment, the watching crowds squatting round him in the sunlight noted it. The word went out; the ruler was no ruler. Soon there would be trouble in distant villages, refusal to pay his taxes and to send him fighting men. If he hesitated again the trouble would grow into revolt. He was autocrat, absolute, but by the will of the people. He must rule by his own mother wit, courage and wisdom openly before his people. If he failed they would reject him.

CHAPTER XXVIII

AS he travelled in the south country his spies brought Ibn Saud news—the desert was a great whispering gallery in which nothing could be kept secret long—that his enemies were again combining against him. Dawish was back among the Mutair and spoiling for revenge. The Ajman were waiting for any chance to raid into Nejd. Husein of Mecca was growing more ambitious. Blown up with his success, puffed up with big ideas—the notables in Syria had suggested that he should call himself King of the Arabs—encouraged by the cousins of Ibn Saud who had taken refuge with him, he claimed all the Ataiba, even those within the boundaries of Nejd itself. He was inciting them to raid. Mubarak was at his old crafty ways, weaving his enemies into a rope to bind Ibn Saud and yet not showing his own hand.

Behind them all were the Turks sending money and men to the Shammar, the Mutair, and to Mubarak, spurring on Husein with promises, collecting troops in Baghdad, and sending soldiers to the Governor of Hofuf, the capital of the Hasa, with orders to help the Ajman against Ibn Saud.

Suddenly there came news that the Constantinople Government was calling back all available troops from Baghdad, Basra, and Hofuf. The Turks had been beaten by the Italians in Tripoli. The Bulgarians had declared war and were advancing on Constantinople. The Turkish Empire was in urgent danger at its centre.

Ibn Saud saw his chance. The Turks as ever were his real danger. The Mutair, the Ajman, the Shammar, and the Rashid, even Husein he could deal with. They were the ordinary problems of Arabia, but the Turks were a Power, and behind them were the Germans; that was another proposition altogether. They would in time eat him up. He would chase them out of the Hasa now while they were weak.

He moved with his habitual caution, kept his intention to himself, and made his plans carefully. The first thing was to verify his information. He sent spies into the Hasa and to Hofuf. They confirmed what he had heard; the garrison of Hofuf and of the coast towns had been reduced; most of the troops had gone north in a hurry.

They reported that the settled population of the Hasa and especially of Hofuf were tired of the Turks. Under them there was no security of property, and no man's life, whether he lived in a village or in a walled town, was safe. The country was full of brigands. All the tribes were turbulent and out of hand. The bedouin raided at will and went unpunished. They would walk into the villages unafraid and take what they wanted. They stole cattle under the walls of Hofuf and even came into the towns and sneered at the Turks. They infested every road and took toll of all the caravans. No one dared be out after dark. No one could travel without an escort, and the escort eat up the traveller with their demand for bribes. Even the short road from Hofuf to the sea was unsafe. Only a few weeks before brigands had raided a convoy on that road, killed the Turkish guard and looted five hundred camels and their loads. Further the Munasir pearl fishers had turned pirates so that no ship dared to come into the harbour at Ojair.

The Turks were helpless. If they sent out soldiers, the bedouins ambushed them and either cut their throats or stripped them naked and drove them home with jeers.

The people would welcome Ibn Saud, said the spies. There were many Wahabis among them. Furthermore the garrison in Hofuf were very slack; they would be easy to overpower; they kept no regular guards; most of them were in the big fort and the rest scattered through the town.

Ibn Saud sent out a call to all his tribes for their contingents of fighting men, saying that he would march against the Murra. As they came in he allotted them to their camping grounds, arranged for their feeding and water, and distributed the camels out amongst the fighting men. When he had some seven thousand he acted.

Choosing a moonless night and turning north and then east he marched at full speed, so as to outpace any messenger who might try to give the alarm, across the Dahna desert into the Hasa and straight at Hofuf.

Taking seven hundred picked men, he went ahead through the oasis which lay thick round the town and halted in the darkness of the palms by the gate of Ibrahim Pasha. A few men with ropes and palm-trunks for ladders crept forward. The moat was newly dug and the town walls were massive, built of blocks of cut sandstone, but in some places in bad repair. At intervals there were towers with sentries in them. Choosing a place where the wall was lower than the rest they waited in the dry moat listening, waiting their opportunity. A sentry from the ramparts above, hearing them, challenged, and getting no reply went on his beat humming to himself.

At once they were up swarming over the wall. Silent on their bare feet some ran to knife the sentries, others to the gate to kill the guard and let in the rest of the men. As yet no alarm had been given, and the town slept quietly.

They made down the market street, the Suq al Khamis, to the fort, a great square building which dominated the town. The gate was open; the drawbridge was down; the sentries and the guard were asleep. Using their knives in silence they rushed the fort. In the darkness and the confusion the unprepared Turks panicked and put up no fight. In a short time the Wahabis had captured the fort and wiped out the scattered detachments.

As soon as daylight came Ibn Saud rode in by the main gate with his standard-bearer in front of him and the main body of his men behind him. The town rose for him to a man. The

Governor and the remnants of the garrison had run for the Mosque of Abrahim and barricaded the doors.

Ibn Saud sent in a messenger with an ultimatum. If they continued to resist he would run a mine under the mosque and blow them all sky-high. They had no chance of resisting or escaping. If they surrendered at once he would let them march away and would guarantee their safety.

The Governor accepted. The next day the Turks marched out with the full honours of war, down to the coast and took ship for Basra.

After that Ibn Saud went through the Hasa receiving the submission of the tribes. He took the ports of Ojair and Qatif and all the coast as far as the boundary of Kuwait and made Jiluwi Governor of the province. The people received him gladly. "The rod of the Saud," they said, "is long. It reaches over the desert and the bedouin are afraid." They hoped for peace and security.

The Turkish Government accepted the position. They could do nothing else. They came to terms with Ibn Saud and made a treaty with him. They recognised the Hasa as part of Nejd and Ibn Saud as the ruler of the whole. They gave him a decoration, money, and arms, and promised that in the future they would not interfere with him. In return Ibn Saud accepted the nominal suzerainty of the Turks.

CHAPTER XXIX

THE conquest of the Hasa greatly increased the importance of Ibn Saud. It gave him a coast-line with two ports, and the English had to consider him when they made their plans in the Persian Gulf.

With success his ambitions had expanded. He did not conceal them. He spoke of them with a flourish of big words. He claimed the south country to the Indian Ocean and that of the Ataiba, away to the Red Sea. He would control Kuwait. He would conquer the Shammar and take all as far as Hail and beyond.

Hitherto all his efforts had been concentrated on fighting, but with material success there began to grow up in him the conviction that what his father had always taught him was true. He had been entrusted by God with a mission.

The Arabs had been a great people ruling a vast Empire founded four square on the religion of Islam. He saw them round him split up with jealousies into sects and races, become of little account and some even ruled over by foreigners and by Christians.

It was his mission to unite them once more in the True Faith of Islam and to lead them back to greatness.

Before, though he had himself lived strictly by the rules of the Wahabis, he had been indulgent with others. The Murra had not disgusted him. He had not resented but rather been interested in the laxness and the irregularities of Mubarak and the people of Kuwait. He had himself bought a gramophone and taken a great delight in it. Now he began to change. He became stricter. Religion became more than ever the basis of all his actions. It was behind his mind in all that he did. He broke the gramophone and forbade any music near him. He would not tolerate laxness in others any more.

A lesser man buoyed up with his success might have become vainglorious and gone conquering at once. Ibn Saud considered calmly. It was true that the Shammar was weak and that Husein had no great force; nevertheless he must consolidate what he had taken before he could expand. He held down his natural instinct to fight and his desire for action. He treated Husein with fair words, though in private he showed how he despised him—Husein, the old dodderer, the agent of the Turks and his Constantinople-bred sons, and especially Abdullah, who was a pestilential fellow.

With Mubarak he kept friendly, called him " Father " : asked his advice and appeared to listen to it, though he knew that the old fox was working against him. The Shammar he left in peace.

From Syria came messengers asking him for help. The new Turkish Government had begun to centralise. It had taken over control of the local governments and was forcing the local people to become Turks. It had extended the Turkish conscription laws to Syria, was calling up the men to serve in the Turkish Army, and had imposed new taxes.

The Syria Arabs were rebellious. Under Sultan Abdul Hamid and the lax rule of the old Empire they had been left much to themselves to run their affairs in their own way. They refused to become Turks : they were proud of being Arabs. They had never served in the Turkish Army and they refused to do so or to pay the new taxes.

All through Syria they were organising revolutionary committees. Their centre was the city of Damascus. They were working to eject the Turks and make an independent Syria, and beyond that a combination of all Arabs into one Empire or Confederacy. They had already been negotiating with Husein and with Mubarak and had obtained their support.

Ibn Saud listened to them. He was as proud as they were of being an Arab. He would allow no Turk to rule over him, but he quickly found that the Syrians were full of empty words. They were dreamers, and their schemes were vague. He wanted facts, something concrete and workable, not a mere blather of words; and he turned back to his own affairs.

His own problem was stability. He held Nejd and the Hasa by the strength of his own right arm and his prestige as a fighter and a ruler, but his people were fickle and unstable. If he weakened or failed, they would turn on him. A small proportion were town and village-dwellers, and on these he could rely; but the majority were bedouin and the bedouin gave no steady allegiance to any ruler. They lived as much by raiding and plunder as by their sheep and cattle. Always on the move, they had no ties to bind them. They were feckless and irrational. They could be turned from tears to laughter and from murder to fantastic generosity with a few words or a twist of fancy. They concentrated on nothing. They were as restless and perverse as the carrion flies.

From his experience Ibn Saud knew that they were useless as subjects and utterly untrustworthy as soldiers. They produced little and destroyed much. They would change side in a battle without warning and loot the defeated. He had punished them savagely, but he knew that though punishment might hold them in check for a time it would not change their characters nor the customs of the desert.

He evolved a plan simple yet so novel that if it succeeded it would revolutionise the whole life of the desert people. He would plant the wandering bedouin in colonies round water and turn them into villagers and cultivators.

His objects were to destroy the nomad and tribal organisation and so break the conventions of the raid and the blood-feud. He would make obedience to God and loyalty to himself greater than loyalty to blood and the tribe. At the same time he would increase the land under cultivation, the man-power of Nejd, and turn the fighting instincts of the bedouin away from killing each other to fighting for him. Success meant stability and power.

He set to work with caution—for there were many difficulties ahead—but with a shrewd knowledge of the character of his people. Religion was the basis of his scheme. By an appeal to religion the bedouin could be roused to great enthusiasm, but only for a short time, for their zeal was like a meteor which flared up white hot for a moment and was turned to dust. Once, however, he had roused their enthusiasm he would tie them to the land with material advantages. First he must get the support of the religious leaders.

Throughout Nejd there already existed a complete religious organisation. In Riad the descendants of the original Abdul Wahab, the preacher who had worked with Saud the Great, formed a hierarchy. Ibn Saud was their Imam, their Leader, and to strengthen his position with them he had married a woman of the Abdul Wahab family who had borne him a son whom he had named Feisal.

From this hierarchy were chosen the ulema, the Doctors of the Law, to whom all religious questions in doubt were put and who were responsible for the carrying out of the religious law and the religious instruction of the people. Under them were all the religious officials, the keepers of the mosques, the *mueddins* who called to prayer and the *mutawas* or preachers, who were distributed through the villages and the tribes in the rough proportion of one preacher to every fifty men. Round each preacher was a school of students.

Ibn Saud set this machinery to work. He talked with his father and obtained his support. The old man had become a recluse. He was pleased to receive guests but, except for public prayer at the mosque on Fridays, he rarely went out of the palace. Though he did not neglect his wives—and even though he was old he was yet virile and his family increased rapidly—he spent all his spare time reading the sacred books and in meditation; so that he had acquired a reputation of sanctity and was greatly respected.

Then Ibn Saud called together the Doctors of the Law in the presence of his father and placed his scheme before them. They listened to him, discussed learnedly and searched the Koran for authority. They were still distrustful of him, that he was too worldly, too ambitious for material success rather than for the service of God.

He dealt with them with quiet tact and restraint. He needed their support. Their perverse reasoning, their crabbed outlook, their ponderous discussions, their everlasting hair-splitting arguments worked on his irritability, but he knew their influence with the people and he listened patiently, persuaded and cajoled them until they turned from distrust to enthusiastic support. His plan became their plan; they would create a fighting brotherhood for the service of God: the bedouin should become the *Ikhwan*, the Brethren united in God.

To the *mutawas*, the preachers, and to the students they sent out orders to go through the tribes preaching against the raid and the blood-feud, teaching that it was grievous sin for Moslem to kill Moslem, that unity to God was greater than loyalty to the tribe, and that the Prophet laid down that it was a good deed worthy of Paradise for Moslems to cultivate the land, and calling for volunteers to form a colony.

At first they got little response. The tribal customs were as old as man and ingrained deep into the character of every bedouin. The desert Arabs were conservative and disliked change. Among the Harb alone there was some response, and Sad ibn Mutib, their sheik, collected some volunteers for the venture, and settled at Artawiya.

Artawiya was a desolate place where there were some wells of good water near the surface which were used by the tribes when grazing and by travellers, and when not in use was covered with brushwood against the sand. Beside the wells were some neglected land and a few uncultivated palm-trees.

Ibn Saud helped Mutib and his volunteers. He came to them personally, encouraged them, brought them a little money and some villagers to show them how to till and to irrigate. He portioned out the land and the water rights, assisted them to build a mosque and some huts of mud and finally watched them take the great step and give up their black goat-hair tents for the huts of the new village.

The experiment started well, and before their enthusiasm could cool off Ibn Saud sent them an Elder with a number of preachers to start a school and to encourage them. Then he sent them a little more money, some seed-corn, and finally he issued a rifle and some ammunition to each man whose name was shown on the register of worshippers in the mosque.

The colony grew. At first there were checks. The colonists were used to the lazy life of shepherds and did not take easily to manual labour. They expected the fields to bear without effort and trusted in God to provide for them, until the preachers spurred them on to work. At another time they became convinced that it was a sin to amass money until again the preachers had convinced them that the Prophet had enjoined on Moslems the virtue of laying up wealth.

Artawiya prospered. It grew quickly from a village into a town. Its inhabitants became the most religious and the most fanatical of all the people of Nejd; they were the fiercest of the

Wahabis, so that no strangers dared to visit them. They foreswore all their tribal rules and customs. They would be held by nothing except the Koran. They discarded the head-dress of the Arabs and wore a white turban as an emblem. They gloried in the name of *Ikhwan*, the Brethren, and all the bedouin became to them ignorant men living in darkness and sin. They were always ready to fight, and their battle cry was " We are the Knights of Unity, Brothers in obedience to God."

More volunteers came in. The Mutair tribesmen caught the enthusiasm. Dawish became one of the Ikhwan and made his peace with Ibn Saud, who appointed him Governor of Artawiya. At first close round Artawiya itself and then in other places Ibn Saud formed the volunteers into new colonies.

He was careful to mix the tribes and inspired them with the fanatic zeal of the first settlers. He connected each colony with the next by ties so that they looked on themselves as all one community, separate from and superior to the tribes of the open desert. As the colonies grew he began to choose his fighting men from among them rather than from the older towns and villages as he had done before.

PART VI

CHAPTER XXX

MEANWHILE throughout the world the British and the German Empires were coming more and more to loggerheads, snarling and growling at each other in every continent and on every sea, massing their tremendous forces against each other.

The Germans, full of young vitality, overcrowded at home, were striving with their ships and their traders and their diplomats to expand. Wherever they went they found that the English already held all that they wanted; and most of all in the Arab countries and the waterways along their coasts. These were the gates and the roads to India and the East; on the one side Egypt, the Suez Canal and the Red Sea; on the other—Mesopotamia and the Persian Gulf. Between them lay Arabia, a threat to both routes.

The Germans found that though their allies, the Turks, were the nominal rulers, the English were in effective control and holding all against them with dogged and resentful pertinacity; and they raged angrily against the English.

To every ruler in Arabia, to the Iman of the Yemen, to Husein the Sherif of Mecca, to the Rashids to Ajaimi, the Sheik of the Muntafik, to Mubarak and to Ibn Saud came emissaries, both official and secret, and from both sides, with promises of gold and good things in exchange for alliances.

To Ibn Saud, from Kuwait, came Shakespeare, the English consul, and from Medina and Basra Turkish and German agents. He listened to them all.

He had a difficult problem before him. He was convinced that a war between the English and the Germans with the Turks was at hand. With which empire should he ally? Or should he not ally with either? He was half convinced that neutrality was his best policy, yet he could not afford to remain isolated, for all round him other rulers were making alliances with one side or the other. He talked with all who came to Riad. He had the newspapers from Cairo, Baghdad, and Damascus read to him, but they gave him little help.

The Turks were the power close at hand. They had behind them the Germans who were rich and strong. They were his enemies. They were allied with the Rashid. They meant to eject him and to control Nejd.

The English were his friends. They did not want Nejd. They wanted to keep open the roads to India and to protect their oil in Persia. They were ready to recognise him as an independent ruler. They too were rich and strong. He had watched them coming up the Gulf from the East. He knew of their rule in Egypt and India, their alliances with Muscat, Hadramaut, Oman, and Aden, their ships, their wealth, and their power. He had seen them warn back both the Turks and the Rashid from Kuwait, and how the Turks had not dared to oppose them even though they had the Germans behind them. He had met and learned to like the English representatives in the Gulf, Cox and Shakespeare. Above all, his father had a profound conviction that the English were the mastermen of the world.

But whereas the Turks and the Germans were within striking distance of him from Basra, Baghdad, and the Red Sea Coast, the English were far away. Their nearest troops were across the sea in India.

He hesitated what to do. He would go and consult with Mubarak. They had common interests in this problem, for if the Germans prevailed and the railway came to Kuwait, it would be an end of the independence of Kuwait as well as of Nejd. He and Mubarak might have quarrelled and sparred during these last few years, but "Mubarak," he said, " has been as a father to me. I will take my difficulties to him."

They met in a village on the frontier between Nejd and Kuwait. Mubarak came with all his usual ceremony, riflemen riding before him, outriders on his carriage horses, and behind him his negro guards in uniforms of blue and gold. He received Ibn Saud affectionately and they sat down to discuss together. On the one side the old man, for Mubarak was old now and had hennaed his white beard and painted his eyebrows to hide his age, a wise old man and very shrewd. On the other, the young man, enormous, restless with energy, very proud, a little boastful and on his dignity, expecting the old man to patronise him.

They talked diplomatically, avoiding their personal differences, discussing only the main question. Mubarak advised avoiding all alliances. With subtle arguments he pointed out the advantages of keeping clear of both the Turks and the English.

He was at his old game. He was jealous of Ibn Saud and his success. He was determined to shut him away back into Central Arabia and to keep him from making alliances. And Ibn Saud was no fool. He realised for what Mubarak was working.

They parted as affectionately as they met, wishing each other all the blessings of God. Inwardly both were angry. Mubarak that the young man was no longer under his thumb. Ibn Saud at the old man's patronising air.

Ibn Saud rode out into the desert back to Riad still undecided.

He could not decide. He sat back and waited on

events, meanwhile bargaining for the best terms from both sides.

He talked with the Turks, sold them camels and horses at good prices. He talked also with Shakespeare and took the money and the arms he offered.

CHAPTER XXXI

AS Ibn Saud, behind the desert, watched, waited, calculated, and parleyed, suddenly far away in Europe came the crash—the World War. For years the rivalries for trade and power among the nations had piled up into monstrous hatreds until all could see the danger and yet the war came without warning and as a thief in the night. France and Russia came hurrying in to crush out Germany. England and a dozen countries followed. Within three months Turkey had declared for Germany and the Turks and the English were at war.

Ibn Saud was caught unprepared. All round him the other sheiks had taken sides and were calling up their men. He found himself, as he had feared, isolated. He sent out messengers suggesting a meeting of the rulers of Arabia: they had no interests in this war, he said, it would be well for them to meet and consider their own interests in common; they might profit largely if they stood together.

He got no response. In Hail a new Rashid had defeated his rivals and was in control. Allied with Ajaimi of the Muntafik he had with his Shammar tribes joined the Turks.

Husein was working with the Turks but at the same time through his son Abdullah coming to terms with the English in Egypt. They had promised him money in sackfuls and arms. He had proposed a scheme, suggested by the Syrian revolutionaries, of an Arab Federation, under his leadership. They had agreed. Anything to get his alliance. The war must be won at all costs. Every possible ally must be bought over.

Flattered by the English, urged on by the Syrian revolutionaries, believing that he would soon be King of Arabia and Caliph of Islam, Husein, puffed up with his big ideas, sent back Ibn Saud a discourteous message: he would have nothing to do with him until he had given up all claim to the Ataiba. He sneered at his heretic Wahabis and his tatterdemalion Ikhwan.

Mubarak, wise, foreseeing, clearheaded, knowing his own mind and the interest of Kuwait had declared for the English. But he was in danger. The English had promised to come quickly but had not yet arrived, and the Turks from Basra might attack him at any minute. He called to Ibn Saud to stand by him. Still Ibn Saud waited. Still it seemed to him that his best policy was neutrality.

In the early winter of 1914 the English landed at Fao at the head of the Persian Gulf, drove back the Turks without difficulty, entered Basra and began to concentrate troops to advance up the Euphrates and Tigris rivers to Baghdad.

They sent Shakespeare to Ibn Saud, for he had become of vital importance to them. As the central ruler in Arabia he could attack outwards either at the Hejaz and the Red Sea Coast or northwards at Syria and on to the Turkish line of advance on Egypt. The Muntafik and the Shammar tribes were threatening the English flank as they advanced on Baghdad. If Ibn Saud could be persuaded to attack the Shammar, that flank would be safe. If, however, he joined the Turks he would be dangerous. Failing active alliance Shakespeare was to try for his friendly neutrality.

Ibn Saud was quite ready for friendly neutrality, but he would not be jockeyed into a treaty. He knew what he wanted. He would take no verbal promises such as seemed to satisfy Husein. He would have a treaty properly set out in black and white or he would do nothing.

As he negotiated with Shakespeare news came in that the Rashid was advancing on Nejd.

The Turks, determined to stop Ibn Saud making an alliance with the English, had given the Rashid money and arms and urged him to act at once before it was too late.

CHAPTER XXXII

IBN SAUD ordered out his fast camel messengers with urgent summons for fighting men. The treaty with the English must wait until he had settled with this danger.

The towns and the villages of Nejd sent him footmen; among these were some companies from the new Ikhwan colonies, on their trial for the first time. The Mutair, the Ajman, and the Dawasir sent him horsemen. As soon as he had assembled three thousand he marched northwards.

He found the enemy at Jarrab which lay to the north of Artawiya and, parking his baggage and camels, he attacked at once.

The battle was fought in the regular desert style. The two sides advanced on each other in long lines, the footmen in the centre chanting their battle-cries, shouting taunts and curses " *Sana-ees*," shouted the Shammar; "*Ahl-al-owja!*" shouted back the Saud's Nejdis; "We are the Knights of Unity, Brethren in God," chanted the Ikhwan. On the flank the cavalry wheeled and galloped in great crowds of dust, looking for a chance to charge in.

Ibn Saud led the Mutair cavalry himself and tore straight at the Shammar horsemen opposite, drove them back, but was unable to hold his men who went chasing the enemy wildly across the desert.

The infantry, firing until they got close, drew their swords and met at the run. From midday until late afternoon they fought hand to hand, a mass of heaving men, hacking, cutting, thrusting, shouting, giving here to re-form elsewhere and crash together again. Now one side gained ground, now the other, until at last the Nejdis were pushed steadily back. The Ajman, seeing this, galloped off and looted the camp and baggage, leaving one flank exposed.

The Nejdis began to give. Ibn Saud rushed in among them, laying about him, urging them on. The Ikhwan stood firm and gave no quarter, but the rest began to lose heart. Keeping them together with difficulty Ibn Saud drew off, but his force broke up, his men made home, the bedouin dispersed, and he reached Riad with only a handful left.

Shakespeare, who had insisted, against Ibn Saud's wishes, on being present, was killed. He had not understood that in desert warfare the art of running and re-forming is the most valuable. When the footmen round him had run and called to him to come he had refused and been cut down by the Shammar camelmen.

The Rashid could not follow up his success. He had been too badly battered. The Mutair had not only scattered his cavalry but looted his camp. He retired to re-form.

None the less Ibn Saud had been severely beaten. Once more the Ajman had betrayed him.

CHAPTER XXXIII

LIKE the wind, the word went out across the desert that Ibn Saud was beaten; the Turks and the Rashid had beaten him. The bedouin passed the news from encampment to encampment away down to the south country. The caravans carried it to Hasa and the Hejaz and up into Baghdad and into Syria. The Ataiba and the Murra in the Great Waste rejoiced; they would soon be rid of this master; the good old raiding days would now come back, they said.

Everywhere the bedouin were on tiptoe to revolt against him. They had grown restless under his firm control, resentful of his refusal to let them raid and loot, and they were suspicious of his attempts, through his preachers and the Ikhwan, to break through their tribal organisations and customs.

Ibn Saud knew his danger. He had little money and few men. He knew that if he showed one sign of weakening he was done. The tribes accepted only a strong man and a successful one. One sign of weakening and they would all rise against him, wipe him out and sweep across Nejd. On every side the world was full of war, and the war fever was in all the tribes. Turkish agents were working through them, distributing gold and urging them to attack him. The Ajman, the accursed Ajman, under their Sheik Hithlain, were already in revolt throughout the Hasa.

But he showed no weakening. He put a bold face on his difficulties. When those round him were fearful and depressed he laughed at them or roared at them in anger, whichever was his mood. He beat a man who brought him bad news. He would hear no bad news. The difficulties and the dangers only keyed him up to greater efforts. He set to work at once, collected a few men from the villages and from the Ikhwan colonies and made as if to attack the Shammar. It was bluff, but it worked, for the Rashid was not ready to fight and agreed to a temporary peace.

Abdullah was among the Ataiba and moving towards Nejd. With fair words and promises Ibn Saud bought him off. Then he looked round for allies. The English were advancing up the Euphrates river from success to success. They had taken the town of Kut and chased the Turks helter-skelter in front of them. They were within striking distance of Baghdad itself.

Ibn Saud hesitated no longer. Clearly the English were winning. He needed their help. He came to terms with the English, and at the port of Ojair in the Hasa he signed a treaty with them. He agreed to stand by them, not to attack their allies or to help their enemies. In return they acknowledged him as the ruler of Nejd, independent of the Turks, gave him a monthly subsidy, some arms and a decoration.

With Mubarak he came also to terms. The Ajman had raided into Kuwait. Mubarak demanded their punishment and that all they had looted should be returned. Ibn Saud agreed, provided Mubarak would help him with men and arms.

With this moral and material backing, taking his brother Sad and Jiluwi and with such men as he could collect, he turned on the Ajman.

His difficulties were great. On all sides his enemies were only waiting to attack him. The Rashid and Abdullah would take the first opportunity. The peaces he had made with them were only "little peaces." In Mubarak's promises he did not trust. He had only a small force, a few villagers with some bedouin horsemen, his bodyguard, and a handful of the Ikhwan.

The Ajman far outnumbered him. He had few camels and fewer horses. It was already midsummer, and the violence of the sun was great. It was not the time for marching and fighting, but he must attack before the revolt spread.

The Ajman were brave fighters. Though treacherous to all else they were loyal to each other and their tribe; and they could put five thousand of the best fighters in Arabia into the field. They hated him bitterly. They now had their chance of revenge.

CHAPTER XXXIV

AS soon as Hithlain heard that Ibn Saud was on the march against him he began to move southwards towards the edge of the Great Waste, into the barren country below Qatar, drawing him after him.

As Ibn Saud got farther south he found little water and less forage so that he had to leave his animals behind, and his men who now had to travel on foot became worn out. They marched only at night as the heat was intense. All day they lay without tents or any protection and scorched by the sun. But he drove them on, for to turn back at this stage would have been as dangerous as a defeat.

At last he found the Ajman in the palm-groves in front of Kanzan and attacked them in the dark. Unknown to Ibn Saud there were only a few of the enemy in front of him. Hithlain had cunningly laid an ambush. His main force was laying off on a flank, and as soon as Ibn Saud was in the palm-groves they swung round on to his rear.

After that there was confusion. Each man fought for himself unable to see in the pitch darkness whether his opponent was friend or enemy. Close beside Ibn Saud his brother Sad was shot dead. He himself was wounded. A bullet hit a pouch full of cartridges in his bandolier. The cartridges stopped the bullet, but he was knocked down by the blow and badly bruised about the ribs. His men, outnumbered and surprised, panicked and ran and with them went Ibn Saud.

He was in real danger. He had his back to the wall. His

prestige was almost gone. In all directions the bedouin were taking heart to turn on him and were raiding. The Ikhwan and the villagers were stout-hearted but too few to hold up a general revolt. The tribes were still strong. It required only a little to break up Nejd into a hundred tribal units raiding and murdering each other as before. The Rashid had ignored his treaty and was advancing on Buraida.

With the few men left to him Ibn Saud remained in the open and kept his mobility of action, but he sent out a general and urgent call for help to his father in Riad, to Mubarak in Kuwait, and to the English. He was fighting for his life.

Fortune saved him. The people of Buraida under Fahad, the new Governor whom he had appointed after Jiluwi, a fanatical Wahabi, turned out valiantly and drove the Rashid back. Husein of Mecca was busy preparing to revolt against the Turks and recalled Abdullah. Hithlain was a stout fighter but no more than a raiding bedouin sheik. He did not pursue Ibn Saud, but turned to looting villages in South Hasa and then began to besiege the town of Hofuf itself.

Abdur Rahman came out of his seclusion, collected a force from the villages round Riad, and sent them off under Ibn Saud's younger brother Mohamed. The English despatched money and arms. Mubarak alone hesitated, and then late in the day sent a small force under his son Salim.

Salim came reluctantly. He was a morose, ill-natured, hard-bitten man with a general dislike of the Wahabis and a personal and bitter hatred of Ibn Saud.

As ever Ibn Saud showed himself at his best in adversity. With disaster close round him he never faltered nor lost heart. His bruised ribs—though none was broken—caused him great pain, but he told no one.

At first the death of Sad plunged him deep down in grief. Out of that grief he came raging back in terrific, blinding anger.

He swore vengeance on Hithlain and the Ajman. He worked with the frenzy of hatred. He had too few men to attack the Ajman direct, but he harried them with quick fierce raids as they sat round besieging Hofuf. He killed without quarter or mercy and counted each Ajman killed as one more to settle the account for Sad. He never stopped. He was always on the move, sleeping even less than before, taking great risks, collecting men from the villages, moving with great speed.

His personality dominated. Tremendous, fearless, intense in his power to persuade and inspire. Once more too his ability to concentrate and persevere to one end and to force his men to do the same carried him through, so that by the time Mohamed and Salim had joined him he had collected a new force.

CHAPTER XXXV

THE Ajman soon grew tired of sitting round Hofuf under the hot summer sun; they wanted loot; the drudgery of a siege wearied them into irritation. Hithlain could not hold them. Many of them dispersed and made for home. The rest eventually gave up the siege and went off raiding.

As soon as he was ready after them went Ibn Saud and having located them he left Mohamed and Salim with the horsemen in camp and made a forced night march on foot, caught the Ajman unawares and attacked them before dawn, himself leading the way, rifle in hand, towering above his men.

The Ajman rushed to their arms and opened fire. At close range a bullet hit Ibn Saud in one thigh and felled him. His bodyguard carried him back, streaming with blood and in much pain. His men, seeing him fall, hesitated and the Ajman taking the chance made to their horses and galloped away.

After them Ibn Saud sent Mohamed and Salim with their cavalry. They caught the Ajman still in full retreat; but suddenly and without warning Salim deserted Mohamed and joined the Ajman.

Once again Ibn Saud was in urgent danger. He lay wounded in his tent. Round him the camp was full of rumours. All his men were downhearted. Some said that the Ajman were advancing again; that more troops were coming from Kuwait to help them. Others that Ibn Saud was done; the bullet had unmanned him; he could lead them no more; he was useless for all time. Without him to cheer and lead them they were like frightened children. Even his best friends, those who had stood by him in the worst times, were wavering. They began to desert; it was best to make for home, they said, while there was still time.

Ibn Saud realised that he must act and quickly. His wound, a deep flesh wound only, was painful but not serious. He would show them that he was not unmanned. He was a man still. He called a sheik of a neighbouring village and bade him find him a girl, a girl and a virgin, fit for him to marry. That night, that very night he carried out the ceremonies and consummated the marriage in his tent in the middle of the camp and ordered all the camp to celebrate the occasion.

It was one of those dramatic gestures of which Ibn Saud was a master. His Arabs, bedouin and villagers alike, were roused from despondency to admiration, and roared their applause. This was a man indeed, a lusty giant of a man who could play lover though he was wounded. From depression they swept up into boisterous, boasting optimism. They would follow him anywhere and against anyone. The position was saved.

He would have attacked the Ajman without further delay. Mohamed was keeping close to them with his cavalry and begging to be allowed to teach them and Salim a lesson. But Ibn Saud hesitated. Salim's treachery justified any action, but to attack him would mean an open quarrel with Mubarak; and he wanted no more enemies at the minute. He sent, however, a note of protest to Mubarak: "Out of respect for you alone, my father," he wrote, "I have not attacked and punished Salim."

Mubarak's reply was brusque. He blamed Ibn Saud. At the same time Ibn Saud intercepted a letter from Mubarak to Salim which ended: "I sent you as an observer, my son Salim, and not as a combatant. . . . If Ibn Saud defeats the Ajman we are with the Ajman, but if the Ajman defeat Ibn Saud do not repulse them, and yet do not aid them.

As soon as he read the letter Ibn Saud flared up: here was the proof of treachery: too long he had borne with Mubarak, his cunning intrigues and his stabbings in the back.

Calling a council he explained the facts. One and all his advisers were for attacking even if it meant war with Kuwait.

"So be it," said Ibn Saud and quoted from the Koran the verse with which it was his custom to declare war: "Thee Oh God, Thee only do we worship and from Thee Alone seek we help"; and gave the orders to break camp and march.

As he set out news came that Salim with his men had left the Ajman and hurried back to Kuwait, for Mubarak was suddenly dead.

"From God we are. To Him we return," said Ibn Saud and marched straight at the Ajman.

CHAPTER XXXVI

IT was a fight to the finish. Ibn Saud could not contain his hatred of the Ajman. He would take revenge on them for Sad. He would punish them for their many treacheries until there was not an Ajman nor a member of the family of Hithlain left. He would make such an example of them that all the tribes should see and never forget it. And the Ajman fought him back with fury.

All through 1916 they fought, now one side winning here and now the other there, until steadily Ibn Saud drove the Ajman back. They were bedouin, fickle and unstable, who wanted only sudden raids and then to go home with the loot, and Hithlain could not hold them together, while Ibn Saud had behind him a solid body of villagers and Ikhwan who stood firm.

The fighting was bitter and brutal. Neither side gave any quarter. The old conventions of desert war were ignored. Wells were destroyed, filled with stones or smashed in. Often it was a race for wells, columns of camels at a steady trot, pouring through the sand-hills like streams, the riders silent, intent, racing the desert for water, knowing that if the enemy got there first they and their beasts died of thirst under the sun; and Ibn Saud and his men moved faster than their enemies.

On both sides the women joined in killing the wounded. A wounded Wahabi pleaded with an Ajman woman to give him a drink and she beat him to death. A wounded Ajman dying beside a well called for a Wahabi woman to help him. She came near as if to help; took his rifle and ammunition and rolled him headlong into the well and went to her village in triumph.

As he drove them back Ibn Saud burnt their villages and killed them without reprieve or mercy. He would listen to no truce. He gave no quarter until those that were left, with Hithlain, ran for safety out of the Hasa into Kuwait. Ibn Saud demanded their surrender so that he might wipe them out and free the country of them.

Jabir, the son of Mubarak, was now sheik of Kuwait, but he was a poor feeble thing and Salim held the power. Salim refused to give up the Ajman. Ibn Saud, not prepared to attack Kuwait —to do so he would have to break his treaty and quarrel with the English—drew off swearing that when the time came he would make a final reckoning with the Ajman and with Salim.

He returned to Riad to find confusion. The minute his control over them had weakened the tribes had come out raiding and fighting among themselves and making all the countryside unsafe. But so soon as he returned victorious they crept home. They recognised him as their master and submitted, and he marched through Nejd re-establishing his authority and prestige.

But whereas with the Ajman he had shown no mercy, with all who made submission to him he was generous and conciliatory. He allowed them to appoint their own headmen and as long as they acknowledged him as ruler and sent him a contingent of fighting men when he called for them, he left them to manage their own affairs.

Once more he was supreme in Nejd.

PART VII

CHAPTER XXXVII

FOR two years Ibn Saud had been struggling for dear life up and down the Hasa and Nejd. He had been submerged in his own troubles, almost swept away and drowned by them and oblivious to all else. Only by immense efforts had he got back to firm ground. But by the end of 1917 he had gained his feet and re-established his position and could look round.

During these two years along the edges of Arabia there had been fierce fighting. A small English army had advanced up the Tigris pushing the Turks in front of it. Before Baghdad it had been beaten back, besieged in the village of Kut and completely captured. A second English army had come from over the seas, organised with more care, advanced and taken Baghdad and was planning a further advance on Mosul.

Out from Egypt another English army had marched northwards, driven the Turks back off the Sinai peninsular, the road into Egypt, and under General Allenby had chased them through Palestine and taken Jerusalem. Allenby was preparing a great offensive against Damascus and beyond that against Aleppo.

Husein of Mecca had declared for the English and was at war with the Turks. At the beginning the English had looked to Ibn Saud, but when he was beaten at Jarrab and all but smashed by the Ajman they realised that for the time being he was of no military value to them. Having made sure that he was ineffectual and having ensured his neutral alliance they had concentrated on Husein.

They had needed Husein as an ally. As Guardian of the Sacred Cities they could use him as a counterpoise to the Turkish Sultan, the Caliph in Constantinople. They could not allow the enemy to control the Hejaz. The Germans were known to have submarines ready to launch in the Red Sea, and from the Hejaz they and the Turks could threaten Egypt, the Suez Canal, and the waterway to India.

The English had determined to get Husein's co-operation at any cost. They had increased their promises and given him twenty thousand gold pounds a month as a subsidy, together with arms and munitions. They had flattered the old man's vanity, promising him his Federation of all Arab Countries with himself as its head. They had realised that such a fantasy might well catch the imagination of the Arabs and bring them out *en masse* against the Turks. The war had to be won by any means. Promises as well as bullets and shells were needed to win it.

And Husein had been willing. The Turks had grown suspicious of him. They had caught and hanged some of the leaders of the Revolutionary Committees in Syria with whom he had been working. He had protested at the executions, and Jemal Pasha, known as Jemal the Butcher, the Governor of Syria, had told him bluntly to mind for his own neck, and then concentrated more Turkish troops in Medina itself.

As soon as he was ready Husein had revolted, repudiating his allegiance to the Turks and declaring himself the leader of a revolt for freedom of all Arabia. In the first rush of enthusiasm his sons Ali, Abdullah, and Feisal with the Hejazi townsmen and bedouin had swept the Turks back and captured Mecca. The Turks had struck back, chased the Hejazi to the seashore and had all but throttled the revolt. Husein and his Arabs beaten to their knees had called to the English for help. In the nick of time the English had sent ships to the ports of Jedda and Yenbo, arms, rifles, ammunition, some guns, gold pieces by the sackful and a handful of Englishmen, among whom was Captain T. E. Lawrence, to help and encourage them.

With these the Hejazi had recovered their spirit; the guns and ships had given them courage; the Englishmen, and Lawrence, had given them leadership; with the gold Husein had hired fighting men from all the tribes, even the best men from Nejd itself.

They had raided up the coast, pinned the Turks down to the railway line, cut the railway between Damascus and Medina, and so isolated the Turks in Medina. Led by Lawrence and Feisal they had captured Akaba and made it into their base and joined up with Allenby's army which was already prepared for its big offensive northwards on Damascus.

On all fronts the English had driven back the Turks and were massing for a great drive to throw them out of the Arab countries. While the Turks, short of food, arms, and ammunition were completely disorganised and dying by the thousand of disease and neglect.

But away in Europe and the main theatres of war the struggle showed no sign of ending or of victory for the Allies. To many neutrals it seemed that the Germans would win.

The English needed every ally they could find. Ibn Saud was once more in control of Central Arabia, and he was of value to them. In haste they sent a mission to him to get his alliance—St. John Philby, a political officer from the Civil Commissioners' staff in Baghdad and with him Lord Belhaven.

CHAPTER XXXVIII

IBN SAUD received the mission with every courtesy. He housed them in his palace in Riad—though the ulema and the people of the town made surly complaints that he talked with Christians and foreigners, unbelievers and infidels. He listened to Belhaven and Philby, but he made no promises. He had made up his mind that for the present neutrality in alliance with the English was his best policy. He would not be persuaded and hustled into action, nor would he allow himself to be used by the English or by any foreigners for their own ends.

Neutrality was profitable as well as a wise policy. The English paid him five thousand pounds a month to remain quiet; good gold was pouring into Arabia from all sides; he could sell camels and horses at a high price; he had a tacit truce with the Rashid to keep the peace so that both might profit by the folly of Europe. The Turks were now far away and little danger to him. Provided they did not come back into the Hasa and Nejd he had little interest in them.

Further, to help the English actively was now to help Husein—and that he would not do. He was not deluded by their talk of an Arab Federation, but even if it was feasible he would not agree to Husein as its head. When he thought of the vast sums the English were paying to Husein and that he was using the money to buy over the tribesmen, even from Nejd itself, he boiled with anger. "You make a mistake," he said to the English mission, "in supporting Husein. As soon as the money stops you will see how I will deal with him and how all the tribes will come back to me."

Belhaven urged him to attack the Rashid in Hail. "Remember," replied Ibn Saud bluntly, "that my friendship with the English has already neutralised the Rashid. I will, however, attack him on the condition that you finance me as you finance Husein; that you guarantee that your allies, Salim and Husein, do not attack me in the back as I advance."

CHAPTER XXXIX

MOREOVER Ibn Saud needed time and leisure to adjust his own affairs. For close on twenty years he had been continuously on the march or fighting.

"I have not," he said in apology to a visitor, " had time all these years to put even my palace in order so that I can entertain my guests with the comfort due to them."

The Ajman revolt had taught him that internal stability was still his most vital need.

He ruled personally. All government and all the administration rested on his shoulders.

He travelled continuously, visiting all parts of the country, saw all for himself, did his work as before, in public before his subjects in direct contact with them.

The tribes accepted him because he was strong. As long as they felt his hand close over them they would be quiet and obedient, but only for so long. The land was not one homogeneous whole, but a hundred broken pieces loosely held together between his hands. There was no machinery or system of government. All stability and security depended on his personal, individual control.

As he conquered more country such personal control became more and more difficult. He took this opportunity, while he had peace, to create a system.

In every town he had appointed governors and sheiks over every tribe, to keep order, to collect taxes, and to muster the levy when called on. Usually he appointed them from some local family with a hereditary standing, but if the people were fractious he sent a man from Riad with a strong bodyguard to support him.

He chose his representatives with care, tested them himself, assessed their characters and so knew how to deal with each—either with an open palm or a clenched fist. He was a good judge of character. He had an instinctive knowledge of men and the motives on which they acted.

When he came to a town he visited not only his governor but all the notables, sat by their hearths with them, drinking their coffee, talking with them intimately so that he learned the local conditions and the personalities round his governors.

With the inefficient, dishonest, and disloyal he had no mercy. He acted at once.

Philby, the English delegate, on one occasion complained that Othman, Governor of Zilfi, was gun-running to the Turks. Ibn Saud had been watching Othman. He knew at once that the complaint was just, and he acted within an hour.

He sent an express messenger with a letter: " Did I not, O thou enemy of God," he wrote to Othman, " forbid thee on oath (to deal with the Turks) . . . and then thou and thy son did purchase food and goods and then didst sit down, thou and he, to profit thereby. . . . This thy evil conspiracy will remain in my memory. Thou art dismissed. . . . Go forth to any country that may be in thy mind except to my countries . . . or else repent and settle under my eye in Riad. If thou delayest, by God! though it be only an hour—verily, I am not the Ruler if there remain a trace of thee and thine left in the land of the living."

And Othman did not hesitate, wait, or argue. He knew the anger of Ibn Saud and was gone with his family within the hour, flying quickly lest a worse thing should come upon him.

Ibn Saud decided to knit all his governors and sheiks into one system under him, and he did this by making each responsible for his neighbours. Thus if a crime was committed in a tribal area the sheik must act and report his action to Ibn Saud. If he failed the sheiks of the neighbouring areas must force him to act and report to Ibn Saud. Only if they failed did Ibn Saud act himself with his Nejdis behind him and then he struck quickly, hard, and without pity, punishing his representatives as well as the criminals so that all feared him.

The system was shrewdly devised. The sheiks and governors had many jealousies and were ready to act as judges and correctors of each other. Ibn Saud knew how to use these jealousies. He had a deep knowledge of his people, their friendships and intermarriages, their blood-feuds and causes of quarrel. He could play the one against the other.

He had moreover a complete intelligence system ready to his hand. In all villages, towns and tribes were the Elders, the preachers and the religious students. Like all devout Wahabis each considered himself the keeper of his neighbour's conscience and judge of his actions, and they were only too ready to pass word of any delinquencies back to Riad.

Thus Ibn Saud was able to keep a firm hand on all the vast country that he now ruled.

PART VIII

CHAPTER XL

IBN SAUD, now in 1917, was thirty-seven years of age and in his prime. A great giant with a handsome head set finely on broad shoulders. He had the easy magnificence of manner of one who has been used to being obeyed and who has long held the powers of life and death over all those round him.

His eyes were brown and full of light. Though they often concealed his thoughts they showed his moods—shrewd and wise when summing up a man or considering a problem, cordial and smiling when he was pleased, and brutal and ferocious when he was angry.

His forehead was high and broad. His features were clear cut and his nose beaked so that, while full-face he gave a sense of repose, side face he had the look of a hawk or an eagle, nervous with energy and on the watch to strike. He wore his moustaches trimmed close and his beard square and short.

Even when seated he was rarely still, but his movements were deliberate and not jerky as those of the ordinary Arab. He walked with long rapid strides. Though over heavy and big for the Arab horses, he sat a horse well and had a great reputation as a swordsman.

Whether at home in the palace in Riad or travelling among the tribes he lived as frugally as if he was campaigning. He cared nothing for comfort. His bed in the palace was a cheap iron affair. His clothes were simple; he used no silk; his only finery was a little embroidery on his cloak and gold wire in his headropes. He was, like many who do not smoke tobacco and who live clean, very sensitive to smells. Unpleasant smells, sweat of bodies, of offal or filth, distressed him. To counteract these he often used scent, especially essence of roses.

Once there came before him a well-known pasha to discuss important affairs of state. The day was hot. The pasha had been eating garlic and onions and he had been smoking—though not before Ibn Saud. For a time Ibn Saud bore with him, but he grew restless with irritation. At last he called to his slaves to bring the incense bowls and perfume the room. After the pasha was gone he burst out angrily:

"Pasha!" he said sprinkling himself liberally with scent, "he was no pasha but a scavenger."

His food was, at most, in the morning some small sweet cakes with curdled milk and in the evening a plate of rice and meat with bread and a handful of dates. Except for coffee and tea which he drank at all times of the day and night, his only drink was water. Even if the weather was cold, as it often was on a winter's night on the plateau, he had no fires in his rooms and no brazier in his tent.

He was always alert, watchful, and working. He slept very little—three or four hours a day. at the most—not because he was a bad sleeper, but because he had trained himself to this allowance by stern discipline, so that he might have more time to work. He grudged each hour to sleep as precious time thrown into the waste of unconsciousness. He had much to do and so short a time in which to do it.

He also worked with great speed and complete concentration. He had a prodigious memory. He would dictate rapidly to two secretaries at once on two different subjects, interleaving his sentences, turning now to one and now to the other, and while he was waiting for them to catch him up deal in broken periods with a judicial case or discuss some matter of business with a minister and keep all clear in his head. An interruption did not muddle him; he would deal with it and then without a question return to what he had been doing before at the point he had left off as if the interruption had never occurred. His brain was never at rest. Even when he was at prayer he was chewing over facts, digesting them and preparing some decision.

In Riad he lived with a certain magnificence. He began to rebuild much of the palace, extending it so that it soon filled a third of the town and he constructed round it a fine wall with towers at the corners and over the gateways.

The audience chamber was a vast room capable of holding three thousand people, with cushions round the walls, the floor covered with carpets and the roof held up by rows of white pillars.

He kept many servants and a large bodyguard. Some of these were enormous negro slaves, the rest were men of Nejd specially chosen. They were dressed in white robes, and sometimes over these they wore gold-embroidered cloaks. They carried revolvers and long carved silver-handled swords. The palace was full of their comings and goings on the errands of the Saud.

In the courtyard there were always large crowds sprawling on the ground or squatting on the benches along the walls, for under the palace were huge kitchens from which Ibn Saud fed a thousand people free each day with great platters of steaming rice and mutton, slabs of flat bread, and bowls of curdled milk.

Under the palace also were store-rooms from which he gave clothes to the needy and presents to his guests. Frugal in his own needs he was lavish in entertaining others and generous to folly. When one of his ministers protested he replied, " Neither I nor my ancestors have ever kept a chest in which to hoard money. Hoarded money does no good. Were the millions of Sultan Abdul Hamid of use to him?"; and again to another, " We reap where we sow. If I sow well in peace and prosperity I shall reap the fruit in war and adversity. In peace I give all, even this cloak "—touching the one he wore—" to any who may need it. In war I ask and my people give all they have to me."

He had an immense pride in his family. He was conscientious in all his family duties. He had married the widow of his brother Sad and adopted his children as a duty. Each day he visited all his family, his children, his sister Nura—his mother had died some years before—his wives in the harem, and sat awhile with his father Abdul Rahman and asked his advice on anything of special importance.

Sometimes if he had finished the day's business early he would, in the cool of the evening, ride out on horseback with his guards, his children and his slaves round him, for a picnic among the gardens and palm-groves outside the town walls.

Once free of the town and its puritan atmosphere he would behave like an overgrown schoolboy, romp with his children, play practical jokes on those round him and roar with laughter if they succeeded, and he was not resentful if they retaliated.

He might start a song, arrange a mock fight with much galloping and shouting and challenge his guards and his brothers to ride races against him or shoot at marks with his rifles. And he would be as depressed if he was beaten and as pleased if he won as if he had been a boy.

Living always at high pressure he was often high strung and moody. Sometimes he was full of good humour and laughter. He loved and would tell a good story. Many of these, as always when the teller and the listeners were all of one sex and unrestrained, were bawdy.

At other times he was morbid with black depression. He chid those round him with little reason. He was then difficult and even dangerous, for he came out of his depression with a burst of terrific anger.

His anger was terrible. It changed the whole appearance of the man, and took possession of him. He vibrated with rage.

But his anger passed quickly; if he had made mistakes he acknowledged them frankly; if he had done injustices he was generous to compensate for them. Mubarak, who never understood him, had criticised him, saying that he was "too quick to anger and too quick to conciliate."

Once Shalub, his chief steward, had made some error. Irritated into a moment of anger Ibn Saud ordered him to walk barefooted, then, at once, that very minute, in the middle of the day, without any preparation, under the violence of the summer sun, across the waterless Dahna Desert to Hofuf.

Shalub was old, fat, and flabby. Leaving his sandals by the door of his master's Audience Chamber he set out, but before evening Ibn Saud had sent camels post haste to fetch him back. He called Shalub to him, sat him down beside him and after talking with him for a while sent him to his house. When Shalub arrived he found waiting for him as a present from Ibn Saud a white-skinned and exquisitely desirable Georgian slave-girl.

Frequently, however, these outbursts of anger were carefully calculated to an end.

Fahad, the son of Jiluwi, was an undisciplined, troublesome, and quarrelsome young blade. One day he struck one of the royal guard. Ibn Saud sent for Fahad. He was sitting in his tent with his secretaries, some of his guards, and Philby the English delegate. As Fahad entered the tent, Ibn Saud was up on to him with one bound and a great bellow, and beating him over the head with his riding-cane. He drove him round the tent in front of him, lashing at him, then thrusting him out through the doorway.

A minute later he sat down beside Philby. He was quiet and cool. He dismissed the incident with a shrug of his shoulders. Fahad and the young bloods should all know that he would not allow any member of the royal bodyguard to be touched by them.

Ibn Saud's private chaplain, one of the ulema, had, from

personal spite, been making trouble among the Ikhwan. Ibn Saud sent for him. The chaplain answered without respect. Ibn Saud drove him headlong out of the room and shouted to his guards to lock him in the common jail, where he kept him for a week in solitary confinement. Just then both the ulema and the chaplain needed a lesson.

When he was depressed this was rarely due to outside facts. Good news certainly elated him, but bad news only braced him to new effort. To grapple with dangers and difficulties did not depress but roused all his fighting instinct.

His depression came from within himself. He was strong and lusty. He had only once been ill when as a boy after the flight from Riad he had rheumatic fever, but he was naturally inclined to be sluggish of liver and he gave himself no chance. He ate his meals irregularly and at top speed and then gulped down glasses of water and hurried off to his work or to some strenuous exercise. He drove himself hard with little sleep, much work, and constant effort. He never rested to recuperate. He was never careful what he ate and drank. When he halted on the march he drank from the first well and after fasting strictly all through the day in Ramadan he would in the evening swallow quantities of fresh fruit. When he was out of sorts he overdosed himself with emetics, pills, and concoctions of the doctors. His whole system rebelled at the treatment and his temper and his spirits suffered.

But, always, whether he was elated or depressed, laughing or angry, there was a part of him somewhere at the back in his make-up, something which cool, calculating, and cautious like a still, small voice steadied him in any decision of importance and held him back from sudden action until, with the labour of thought, he had reached a sound judgment.

CHAPTER XLI

LIKE most great men of action, Ibn Saud delighted in talk and discussion. Talk crystallised his thoughts out of vague, nebulous uncertainties which skirted just beyond the reach of the mind, into facts and hard decisions. Talk brought him into direct contact with other minds.

In his affairs the spoken word was more important than the written. He dealt with problems directly with the men who presented them and not through documents. He judged cases facing accused and accuser and without reference to old memoranda, papers or legal tomes. News, reports, petitions all came to him by word of mouth. The spoken word, the tone of the voice, the manner and personality of the speaker were the deciding factors.

After a day's work, talk and discussions were his relaxations, for the ordinary relaxations, music, dancing girls, drinking, and cards were all forbidden. It was his habit after the evening prayer to hold a general council. After that for a while he visited his harem and then he would call his friends and guests to his private apartments.

There he would talk of all manners of things, people, horses, camels, falcons, hunting, war, his past fights, religious problems. Above all he enjoyed calling any foreigners who might be in Riad and hearing of the doings of the outside world and of international politics.

He would sit on a high divan with his legs and bare feet curled under him, his robe drawn round him and his head-ropes laid aside.

As he talked he would pause for a minute with his hands on his knees, looking ahead of him, his chin and short, stiff, black beard thrust forward, thinking out and choosing his words. He would speak in a clear tenor voice that was mellow and soft in ordinary talk, but when he was excited or angry rose and rang out like a trumpet—in sonorous phrases and with expressive gestures.

His hands were enormous, each one as big as two of any ordinary man, with long tapering fingers and very expressive in gesture. With a shiver of a hand he would show how a dying man fought for his last breath or with a roll of his wrists how a column of camels moved and swayed on the march through sand-dunes.

Sometimes for half an hour he would talk without a break, now working himself up into a passion, now lowering his voice with earnestness, using his hands, his shoulders, his whole body in eloquent gestures.

Though he needed little or no sleep, yet as the hours crept by often his guests grew drowsy and sleep bore down their eyelids with its weight. Ibn Saud would watch until perhaps one would tuck up a leg beneath him, spread his hand open before his face to hide himself and doze off, when he would explode a question at him. " So ! Ahmed, is it not so ? Tell us the facts ! " and the sleeper bemused would wake with a start, keep his seat with difficulty and pretend that he had not slept. At which Ibn Saud would chuckle with delight and bait the sleeper.

Such jokes amused him. It happened that one day there came to see him a bedouin sheik named Nafi ibn Fadliya, who was well-known for his greed and his shamelessness. He complained that while he was poor, Ibn Saud was wallowing in riches and comfort, and suggested that Ibn Saud, to level up some of the difference between them, should give him one of his slave girls.

" Go," said Ibn Saud, " to the harem and chose a girl who will please you," but he kept the sheik talking while he sent word to the women how to receive him.

When the sheik climbed the stairs to the harem, panting with excitement to make his choice, the slave-women met him at the top and with kicks and cuffs and blows chased him down to the bottom where Ibn Saud and a great crowd waited for him, splitting their sides with laughter to see him running for safety from a pack of women.

Often Ibn Saud would talk a whole night through. Now and again he would call for his black slaves to bring coffee and tea until, as night paled into the false dawn and the stars over the desert began to die in the morning sky, he would send for more tea and bowls of *laban*, curdled camel's milk, and after he had made his guests eat and drink he would conduct them with majestic ceremony to the door and send his slaves to see them safely home.

While they crept wearily to bed he would, fresh and vigorous as if he had slept, in the cool before the dawn, climb to the roof of the palace and, as the mueddins from the mosques began to call and the town below him woke, look to Mecca and say the Morning Prayer. After that he would go to his rooms where his secretaries would have prepared such work as was urgent, ready for him to decide.

CHAPTER XLII

BY the spring of 1918 Ibn Saud had a firm hold on Nejd, but his relations with his neighbours had become so complicated that it needed all his skill and self-control to steer a good course.

The Rashid was quiet for the time being. He was doing a fine trade with the Turks. He had an arrangement with Salim, who was now sheik of Kuwait. Salim, twisted and black-hearted as ever, was playing a crooked game. Allied with the English and under their protection he was landing goods of all sorts and transporting them by caravan through the Rashid to the Turks in Damascus.

Salim was to Ibn Saud like a blister on a sore lip. He had not forgiven him his treachery over the Ajman. He threatened him. He swore that, when the chance came, he would plant his flag inside Kuwait town. He cut across his contraband trade and held up his convoys. Salim retaliated by encouraging the Ajman to raid into Nejd and by imprisoning Ibn Saud's men if they came into Kuwait.

Between Ibn Saud and Husein the quarrel had become very bitter. As the Turks were driven back by the English, Husein grew more and more high-handed. He strutted about blown out with fantastic meglomania.

Eventually he proclaimed himself "King of the Arab Countries" and wrote demanding that Ibn Saud should recognise his new title and forthwith give up his claims to the tribes of the Ataiba.

The wording of the letter was offensive, and when Ibn Saud read it he flew into a passion and cursed Husein, but he held his hand. The time was not yet come for action. He realised, however, that soon he must fight Husein and he prepared. He sent out his preachers, the fanatical Wahabi *mutawas*, among the Ataiba to convert them to be Wahabis and to set them against Husein.

The preachers had much success. Many of the Ataiba listened to them. The people of the town of Khurma under their headman Luwai, who had quarrelled with Husein, became Wahabis, threw out Husein's representative, refused his taxes, and placed themselves under the protection of Ibn Saud.

Khurma was an important town. It stood in a rich oasis, surrounded by palm and tamarisk-groves and fields of corn and lucerne. It was a trading centre where the bedouin of Nejd came to exchange their sheep and wool with the merchants from the Hejaz. Above all it was the key to the Hejaz, for it controlled the roads into the heart of Husein's country, to his port at Jedda, to his summer residence in Taif, and to his capital in the sacred city of Mecca.

Husein could not allow Khurma to remain in the hands of his enemy. He sent eight hundred men to retake it, but the townspeople were stout-hearted. The majority of them were negro freedmen. Calling on the neighbouring bedouin to help them, they beat off Husein's men, chased them through the palm-groves, across the dried-up river bed that lay to the west of the town, and out into the plains beyond.

Throughout Nejd went up a growl of anger. The Wahabis and Ikhwan demanded to be led out to defend Khurma against Husein. "It is the Sherif Husein who is our enemy," they said. "He is a heretic. It is a scandal that such a one should be Guardian of the Sacred Cities. He is a traitor and a usurper. It is shameful that he should attack True Believers and Wahabis and go unpunished. Up, O Abdul Aziz, and lead us at him."

"Yea," replied Ibn Saud. "It is true. Husein and the people of Mecca are *muskribin*, heretics. They are an abomination that stinks in my nostrils, but for reasons of state I must wait awhile."

CHAPTER XLIII

IN reality Ibn Saud was in a cleft stick. All his instincts, his desires, his pride, and his people urged him to attack Husein, but always at his elbow was the English mission with Philby demanding that he remained loyal to the treaty he had made with England. Husein was the ally of England, they said, it would be a breach of the treaty to attack him. They urged him instead to attack the Rashid, the ally of the Turks and the common enemy. Belhaven talked of Damascus, suggested that he should strike there, but Ibn Saud knew his limitations. He would not over-reach himself with vain ideas. He put the suggestion behind him without hesitation.

But all that summer Ibn Saud was pulled this way and that, unable to decide which road to take. He was in a fever to attack Husein, but if he did, he would have to quarrel with the English, for it would help the Turks. He did not wish to quarrel with the English. He was convinced that they would win the war, and all his spies reported that the Turkish armies were about to break. Half-starved, crippled with disease, short of arms, and without organisation or spirit their men were deserting so that there were more deserters than soldiers in the ranks. Whereas the English were bringing up fresh troops, guns, armoured cars, and aeroplanes and massing to attack.

"Verily," he said with a sigh, "verily if it were not that an open breach with Husein would be against the English and would help the Turks there is none I would sooner attack than

Husein, for I hate him, and as for Abdullah his son he is a poisonous fellow."

As he hesitated things grew worse. Husein sent another force against Khurma. Again they were driven off. Again Luwai of Khurma called to Ibn Saud for help and Ibn Saud sent him none.

Instead he wrote a letter of protest to Husein, who returned his letter unopened with an insulting message given in public verbally to the messenger, to tell Ibn Saud that he, King Husein, would march on Riad and wipe out Ibn Saud and his heretical Wahabis.

The people of Riad and Nejd began to mutter against Ibn Saud. The Ikhwan joined in. The muttering grew from a growl of indignation into a roar. His father, his advisers, the ulema, the sheiks led by Dawish of the Mutair and his Ikhwan all demanded that he attacked; but the English mission was still at his elbow holding him back.

Moreover, he could not understand the English and their policy. They were allied with him and yet they protected Salim of Kuwait who sent the Ajman raiding against him. They urged him to attack the Rashid, and yet let Salim send arms to the Rashid to use against him. They held him back from attacking Husein and gave Husein money and arms and with these Husein sent men to fight him.

And Philby was in no position to explain how in the rush and turmoil of war the various departments of the English Government, the India Office, the War Office, the Foreign Office, the Arab Bureau in Egypt, all parts of one machine had each made separate and conflicting treaties and were working in different ways and often in hostility to each other. For the India Office was allied with Ibn Saud and gave him money and arms, while the Arab Bureau had allied with Husein and given him money, arms, and promises, and the Foreign Office had signed treaties with the French in conflict with both the others.

CHAPTER XLIV

AT last Ibn Saud's patience began to break down. Complications always irritated him. He sought always to reduce a problem down to its simplest essentials and make a clear decision. He hated to be undecided. Indecision was a pain and agony of mind to him.

On one occasion Philby had involved him in a complicated argument with no end. Polite for a while, eventually Ibn Saud bridled up. He swept Philby's arguments aside. " By God," he declared impatiently and beating his walking-stick on the ground to emphasise what he said, " By God, I do not weary myself with such speculation. I have enough to do to rule this land righteously in the fear of God until my time comes to die." That was his philosophy of life.

But his relations with Husein and the English refused to be simplified. He could not make up his mind, and his indecision made him irritable and out of temper.

Moreover, the month of Ramadan, of the Great Fast had begun. In ordinary times the Fast was a trial of the flesh, but that year it fell in June and was a penance that mortified mind and body. All day from sunrise to sunset he and all his people fasted, neither eating any food nor drinking ; some of the strictest would not even swallow their own spittle. Only at night could they eat and drink and satisfy themselves with their women.

Ibn Saud slept as little as usual, three or four hours at most. All through the parched and dusty summer's day while the heat and the glare beat down making a furnace of the palace and while even the Ikhwan slept to pass the empty hours and stifle their thirst, he worked, held his councils, did justice, heard complaints, and prayed the regular five times.

But the strain told on him. He rounded on Philby who was always there, as persistent as a summer fly, protecting Husein and urging him to attack the Rashid. " On all sides the allies of the English threaten me. May God cut them off," he said, using what was for a Wahabi a strong oath, for the Wahabis, unlike the Arabs of Egypt, Syria and Mesopotamia, whose mouths are full of blasphemy, rarely swore. " Yet I also am an ally of the English, and still they threaten me. But be minded of this, O Philby ! if the English will not protect me from their allies I will defend myself."

But he began to lose grip. He was ill, tired, irritable and unreasonable. The English who saw him were surprised how he had lost his fire and self-confidence ; how he looked bowed and troubled ; how he would talk for hours without sequence and without reaching conclusions.

He was growing unpopular. There was a feeling that there was no leader. The Wahabis were getting out of hand. Husein had sent yet a third force to Khurma and been driven back, but was preparing a big force with artillery to crush the town.

The people of Khurma had sent more messengers to Ibn Saud. They had sent some of the spoils of the victory, a field-gun, a Turkish automatic rifle to show what they had done. Finally they had sent him an indignant message : " If it is for the dross of the world's treasure you seek and that you come not to help us, O Abdul Aziz," they said, " then tell us. We will excuse you. We have had no benefit for our frequent sending of men to implore your assistance, but next time we will send our women to raise all Nejd to help us."

The message was known throughout Nejd and roused a storm. The ulema, more ill-natured than usual as a result of fasting, criticised Ibn Saud publicly in the General Council. Sheik Abdul Wahab, the High Priest of Riad, spoke very bitterly saying that Ibn Saud was neglecting the interests of Islam and his own people ; he was being led by the nose by the English ; it was clear that either they could not or would not check Husein ; the people of Khurma had spoken of the " dross of the world's treasure " and they had meant the English gold, and rightly. He was selling his birthright for a mess of pottage.

The Wahabis protested against the English being allowed in Riad at all. If a Wahabi met one of the mission he averted his eyes, turned aside, and spat. The Arab servants of the mission were boycotted.

Ibn Saud could not quiet his men by force or persuasion. Dawish was talking of war and the Ikhwan were arming. They told him categorically that unless he would lead them out they would themselves declare war on Husein and march to help Khurma and capture Mecca without him. He could hold them no more. His grip was slackening.

Suddenly came news that Husein had agreed with the Rashid and Salim of Kuwait to make a concerted attack on Nejd. Husein was collecting men. Salim was egging on the Ajman. The Rashid had called out the Shammar and given them a rendezvous.

CHAPTER XLV

AT once Ibn Saud put out his hands and took a fresh grip. Indecision, like a load that bows a man's shoulders and drags his feet, had feebled him. He threw it away from him with an angry growl and opened his shoulders. The labyrinthine uncertainties, the wrestling and arguing with himself, the hours of formless talk were finished. He was decided. He had made up his mind. He would attack the Rashid and at once.

He need not quarrel with the English. They would in fact give him more arms and money to go against the Rashid. He could divert the war-fever of the Wahabis and the Ikhwan. He could hit indirectly at both Salim and Husein through the Rashid.

Getting a promise from Philby that the English would keep both Salim and Husein from attacking his flanks he sent his eldest son Turki, with a body of the best Ikhwan fighting men and Dawish as his adviser, to harry the Shammar tribes and hold them back.

Next he turned to Sheik Abdul Wahab and the ulema. He swept them along with the vigour of his arguments, over-riding their objections—the Rashid, the hereditary foe, the old enemy who had ruined Nejd before, was still the arch-enemy, he said, and behind him he had the Turks; they were giving him ten thousand gold pieces a month and arms; they had promised to make him " The Sultan of Arabia." All Nejd knew what the Turks and the Rashid would do if they came again to Riad. As to inane old Husein, the Sherif, he could wait; he could be dealt with easily when they had time; the English would keep him quiet for the time being; there was nothing to fear from him; but the Rashid was a pressing danger; he had called up his fighting men; his Shammar tribesmen were already on the move; he was only waiting for a fresh consignment of arms from the Turks before he attacked; they must advance straight at him before he was ready.

Having won over the ulema he sent out a call for a general muster of leaders to meet him before the town of Shaqra.

They came eagerly; they wanted war. As the contingents arrived Ibn Saud greeted them and allotted space where each sheik and headman pitched his camp with his banner and spear planted before his tent and his followers with their camels and horses grouped round him.

When there was a multitude assembled he called them to conference. The townsmen, villagers, bedouin, and a great company of Ikhwan squatted round making three sides of an immense square in the open sandy plain beyond the northern gate of the town. On the fourth side, with his guards round him, sat Ibn Saud. As he told them that the war was with the Rashid and the Shammar they became morose and suspicious.

First one spoke and then another. They were opposed to war with the Rashid, but eager to fight Husein or the Ajman. Then the Ikhwan put forward Dawish of the Mutair as their spokesman. "We demand," said Dawish, "to fight either the Sherif Husein whom the English have armed and who threaten our Brethren in the Faith in Khurma, or to attack the Ajman who, protected by the English, are for ever raiding into our land and escaping back with loot and without punishment. All we want," he concluded, "is to attack the foes of the Faith. Give but the word and we will follow you to death, O Abdul Aziz, against the Sherif Husein or against the Ajman."

Ibn Saud sat listening to them all. He understood what was

in their minds. They had been told that he was allied with the infidel Christians, with the English, and that this war was at the orders of the infidels for the profit of foreigners. He was on dangerous ground and needed all his skill. To one side sat Dawish, the bristling, stiff-necked old raider who resented the checks Ibn Saud put on his raiding and who hated all foreigners and especially the English, a jealous, crafty man, and his opponent though he hid what was in his heart.

Behind Dawish were the rows of Ikhwan, awkward, sullen, and fanatical. They had become a power in the land these last few years; their numbers had increased greatly; they formed the bulk of his fighting men. He must win them to him now. A false move and their hatred of foreigners would flame out in uncontrollable fanaticism. Dawish would fan the flames and they would sweep him aside and attack Husein against his orders.

For a while he remained silent, thinking, with his eyes cast down, his hands on his knees, motionless, and the great square of men under the red August sun with the desert stretching away behind them remained silent, watching him, waiting for him.

He ran his hand over his beard once or twice and suddenly shot out an arm and spoke, facing them, his face alight. He knew how to handle these men. He understood how to get into their hearts and convince and rouse them. He had all the art and personality of a great orator to reach out to them and fill them with himself. He talked to them now with honeyed words, now called to their religion, fired them with belief in himself, summoned them to gird up their loins and fight for the Faith. "Look you," he said, raising his voice gradually until all could hear him. "You are my army in that I have no army nor strength save in God and you. . . . Think not that I am unmindful of what is necessary, and as for the Sherif, think no more of him. Either the English will stop him from attacking Khurma again or—and I give you my word on that—I myself will march against him. . . . All I need do is to send a member of my family or just a slave and the whole south will rise against the Sherif. And as to the Ajman you do not know of what you talk when you say that the English are supporting them. Why the English say to me, ' You are foolish. You have the means. Strike now at Hail.'

" They are right. I have the means to strike, and yet I dally. Of what account would be the Ajman if I held Hail ? If I were master there the English would leave all the desert tribes to my rule and we should have no more trouble from those who sit on the borders of our land."

After that he explained to them that the Rashid was the real enemy ; he appealed to them to trust him and place their hands in his. Then he called on the ulema present to stand forward and give their opinions and one and all they agreed that the Rashid was the enemy of the Faith.

The Ikhwan, swept from sullen suspicion to passionate agreement, shouted out their approval and they beat their foreheads on the ground and wept and cried, " O Abdul Aziz, why did thou not trust in us before and we would have fought for thee without suspicion."

Once more Ibn Saud was their trusted leader. The tribesmen crowded to his tent, to touch his hand in fealty.

At evening they made two long lines in the desert behind the camp and in the centre of the front line as Imam, as the Leader, towering above them all, stood Ibn Saud. Behind him, taking no part in the prayers, was a negro, with a drawn sword, guarding him against a chance enemy.

All took their time from Ibn Saud, prayed in unison, did their obeisances to Mecca, chanted the " Amens " in answer to his invocations as he recited the opening chapter of the Koran.

" Praise be to Thee, O God, Creator of the Worlds, The Beneficent, The Compassionate, Lord of the Day of Judgment. Thee only do we worship, and Thee only do we beseech for help.

Guide us on the right path, the path of those Thou hast blest, not of those with whom Thou art displeased, or of those who have gone astray."

After that Ibn Saud turned to them. "Get you gone every man to his house," he said. "Haste! Make ready for war! and having set your houses in order meet me at Buraida at the new moon and, God in His Mercy, will give us victory."

CHAPTER XLVI

A MONTH later, leading the vanguard himself Ibn Saud made a forced march on Hail. His spies had located the Rashid raiding away to the west and the town was poorly defended.

Between Ibn Saud and Hail were the shepherd tribes of the Beni Yatraf, and being loyal to the Rashid they resisted stoutly.

Driving into them Ibn Saud flung them aside, but the delay was sufficient to warn the Rashid who hurried back into Hail, shut the gates of the town, and prepared for a siege.

Ibn Saud did not want a siege. The Shammar had plenty of fight in them. His tribesmen grew restless if forced to sit round a town. They had taken good loot, animals, arms, and some gold from the Beni Yatraf and wanted to go home. He had done what he set out to do, taught the Rashid and the Turks a lesson, frightened Salim, and broken up the confederacy against him and for the time being satisfied both the English and his Wahabis.

The Rashid asked for peace. Ibn Saud agreed and having divided the spoil marched home in triumph.

CHAPTER XLVII

AS Ibn Saud marched back from Hail to Riad the English under Allenby in Palestine and Maude in Baghdad advanced driving the disorganised Turks before them.

Feisal and Lawrence with their Arabs swept along one flank and with Allenby entered Damascus and pushed on northwards to Aleppo, while Maude took Mosul. Together they thrust the Turks out of all the Arab countries over the Taurus mountains. Bulgaria and Turkey prayed for an armistice. Austria followed. Rotted through by gnawing revolution Germany caved in like a worn shell. The World War was over.

On the heels of the War came the Great Influenza Plague of 1918. The disease bred out of the bodies of the starved peoples of Russia and Germany, matured by the agony and strain, torn men, filth, litter of unburied corpses on all the fronts, mildewed fields, the fear and despair of millions in all Europe, came creeping, insidious, gaining strength as it came, uncheckable, relentless, across the world, a pestilence killing more men than the War itself.

It swept across Arabia. It decimated the bedouin and the villagers of Nejd. It burst into Riad, smote the townsmen, taking the strong before the weak until there was a death in every house. In the palace it killed Turki, Ibn Saud's first-born, a gallant brave youth, his heir and the apple of his eye; and in the royal harem it killed Jauhara, his Queen.

While all Riad lamented its dead, in the palace Ibn Saud sat alone, mourning. He had married many wives, but Jauhara had been the only woman he had loved. She had been his cousin and a princess of the Saud family. His mother had arranged the marriage many years before. Ibn Saud had been a young man then, still fighting for his bare existence against the Rashid, and Jauhara had been but seventeen.

She had been beautiful and talented far beyond the ordinary Arab girl. He had fallen passionately in love with her. Once they had quarrelled and parted for a while, but very soon he had known that he could not live without her and she had come back to him. She had borne him two sons. The years had only increased his passion for her. He had made her his Queen.

All his life Ibn Saud had enjoyed women, women as wives and companions, women as mothers of his children. He was happy with women round him.

He made no secret of the fact. He had nothing to conceal. He had no abnormal vices. These hardly existed among the desert people. If a man sought such lecheries he must go to the great cities of other countries. He had had many wives. He made no apologies and explanations for them, for he had broken no conventions thereby.

He did not need any excuses. He observed the principles of his religion. "I follow the Prophet, the Peace of God be upon him," he said. "What he sanctions I take. What he enjoins I obey. My wives shall always be to the full number that he has allowed."

One day in 1917 when talking to Belhaven he had expressed his surprise that in enlightened England adultery and fornication should go unpunished—in the desert the penalty for adultery was death by stoning and for fornication public flogging—and that they should be even gloried in and praised in books and poems. Belhaven piqued, retaliated, "How many women have you had?" he asked.

"I have four wives as the Prophet allows," replied Ibn Saud.

"But how many have you had and how many have you divorced?"

"I have married and divorced a hundred, and if God wills I shall marry and divorce many more," he replied.

On another occasion he was talking with Philby on marriage and divorce. "By God," he said, "in my lifetime I have married many wives, and by the Grace of God I have not done with wiving yet. I am still young and strong. And now with the losses of the War assuredly the time will come when the people of Europe will see wisdom, and the men take more wives than one each."

He could not understand a man having only one wife. It was unreal, a subject for jest. Such a man was to pitied. He should go to the doctors and be revived.

He lived strictly and devoutly by the rules laid down by the Prophet. Christ had given no instructions for the number of wives for Christians. Mohamed claimed to complete the revelation of Christ and had laid down:

"Thou mayst take two, three, or four wives, but no more."

He gave wives a high position, special rights of property, alimony, and ordered that they should be treated well, saying:

"If thou canst not deal equitably and justly with each and all thou shouldst take only one;"

but he made divorce easy.

It was Ibn Saud's custom to keep three wives and the fourth place empty so that he could fill it as he wished. If there was no vacant place when he needed one he divorced to make the vacancy.

He kept no concubines, had no forbidden liaisons or illegitimate children. He treated his wives well and kept them in state. Each evening after he had prayed and finished the day's work, towards nine o'clock, he went for a while to the harem, and no wife ever complained that he neglected her.

He married for many reasons. Sometimes they were political so as to strengthen his position by alliances with important families, as when he took a girl from the family of Abdul Wahab in Riad to link himself with the religious leaders. He had a wife from the Sudair, another from the Mutair, one from the Anaza tribe, another from the Dawasir. One by one he married into all the leading families. They did not resent the divorces, which carried no stigma, and roused no ill-feeling. It was an honour that one of their women had been married with the Saud. If she bore him children there was a direct bond of blood.

Moreover, Ibn Saud looked after the women he divorced, gave them money and found them new husbands if they were childless and if they were mothers of his children accepted them and gave them slaves and a house in which to bring up the children.

Sometimes again he married to cement the loyalty of a tribe newly conquered, or to give a family that had fallen on evil days and which he desired to raise, a new position or because it was his duty as when he married the widow of his dead brother Sad.

But he married also because being a vigorous, healthy man he desired women. He loved a good fight, a good song, and he was a tremendous lover.

Nevertheless through all the complications of his life and despite all the women who came to him, during the many years of their marriage Jauhara had been his one woman. She was his Queen.

The death of Turki nearly broke his heart. For Jauhara he mourned long. Her death for a while obliterated all else. All that late winter and the first days of the spring of 1919, which were wild and beautiful with fresh sunshine and bursts of rain sweeping across the plateau of Nejd, Ibn Saud mourned and would not be comforted. He saw no one. He shut himself away alone. He closed the rooms where Jauhara had lived in the palace, leaving all untouched as she had left them, and, except for his sister Nura who governed his household for him, he allowed no woman to enter them.

He kept her slaves and servants and every Friday after the Morning Prayer he made a pilgrimage to her grave in the great cemetery of Riad.

CHAPTER XLVIII

OUT of the shadow of grief Ibn Saud was forced back into life by the need of action.

Abdullah was on the move against him. Hitherto Abdullah and his men had been besieging Medina where the Turkish garrison under Fikri Pasha had still held out. Even when the Armistice with Turkey had been signed Fikri Pasha had refused to give in. But early in 1919, cut off and surrounded, short of food, without any hope of relief, his men dying of disease, he surrendered.

Forthwith Abdullah marched into the Ataiba country to force the tribes to submission and to recapture Khurma.

Ibn Saud took up the challenge. He was glad of action, glad to be up and doing and not sitting thinking. His patience too was at an end: the ulema had been right when they had said that either the English could not or would not hold Husein and his son. At Shaqra he had sworn to the Ikhwan to defend Khurma if it was again attacked. He would go to the help of Khurma.

This time he had no difficulties. Men came flocking in to his call, eager, shouting to march to the defence of Khurma and of their Wahabi brethren against Husein, the heretic, the apostate, the traitor who had sold his people to the English.

The English in Egypt offered to arbitrate. Both Ibn Saud and Husein continued to prepare, but whereas Husein did it openly with much boasting, Ibn Saud with greater wisdom acted quietly. He would let Husein take the offensive and put himself in the wrong.

The English held a conference in Cairo. Husein had been their active ally in the war. He would still be useful in peace. Whereas of Ibn Saud they thought little. At most he was a successful tribal sheik of the Inner Desert. They were sure that Husein with his English-trained army, his Syrian officers, and the rifles and machine-guns which they had given him would easily drive Ibn Saud back to where he belonged, to the Inner Desert, out of the way.

They decided to support Husein. They warned Ibn Saud back. They ordered that he restore Khurma to Husein. They threatened that if he advanced farther they would " render to King Husein all assistance " in their power. Further they threatened to reduce or cut off his gold subsidy if he did not listen.

" Success," replied Ibn Saud with dignity, " comes from God alone. I do not deserve to suffer the loss you threaten . . . but if you decide to cut off the subsidy, God be Praised, my honour will remain untarnished. I shall be free to act according to the dictates of my honour."

CHAPTER XLIX

WITH the full sympathy of the English, Abdullah with four thousand regular troops armed with modern rifles and machine-guns and ten thousand bedouin marched on Khurma and halted at the village of Turaba. Ibn Saud was already at the wells of Sakha to the east. Both were converging on Khurma when Luwai, the headman of Khurma, acted on his own.

Khurma was full of Ikhwan volunteers. Spies had brought word to Luwai that Abdullah had pitched camp in the oasis beyond Turaba and had neither taken any precautions nor even posted sentries. It was already late May: the moon was in the third quarter and the night dark. There had been a rainstorm and a low mist increased the darkness.

Luwai made a sudden night march and attacked. He caught the enemy asleep, the officers undressed a-bed. The Ikhwan rushed the camp meeting with no resistance. They killed silently with their swords and knives, taking no prisoners and giving no quarter.

Abdullah ran for a horse and galloped away to safety in his night-shirt without stopping until he reached Mecca and ran, still in his night-shirt, pell-mell into the palace, straight up to his father, shaking and jabbering, with all the boast frightened out of him. The bedouin melted away or deserted to Luwai. Of the four thousand regular troops only a hundred escaped: all the rifles, machine-guns, tents, and stores were captured. The army of Husein had ceased to exist.

As soon as the news was out the people of Taif ran for safety. Mecca was at that moment full of foreign pilgrims who fled down the road to Jedda and demanded to be shipped away. The terror of the Wahabis and the Ikhwan filled all the Hejaz. Husein, stout-hearted but hysterical with anger, cursed Abdullah and sent frantic messages to the English for help.

Ibn Saud with his main body marched into Turaba. He walked across the battle-field exulting. All the country round was strewn with corpses and litter of tents and stores which had been looted: his enemies had been destroyed and not by his army but by an unorganized crowd of his Ikhwan. His Ikhwan had shown their fighting metal. Before him the road to Mecca lay open. Husein and all the Hejaz were at his mercy.

CHAPTER L

AS Ibn Saud prepared to advance the English again warned him back. He calculated quietly: Turaba had been an easy victory and the excited Ikhwan were shouting to be led on to Mecca: he hated Husein: he desired revenge: to conquer the Hejaz, the Sacred Land of Islam, was his ambition; the road ahead seemed open and without obstacles. His advisers urged him on. They even hinted at his lack of courage to seize the chance, but he would not be hurried or bustled. He considered coolly.

It was an ability, this steady self-control, this power to judge and value facts in their real proportion, to remain cool and critical even in the heat and turmoil of great events when those round him were in a frenzy of excitement—an ability which had many times saved him from error and disaster.

He saw clearly the tremendous power of the English. As conquerors in the World War, they stood astride the whole East and Middle East holding all in their grip. He realised that they meant to support Husein; and he realised that at the moment he could not fight the English.

He had now for many years been an absolute ruler and surrounded by men, afraid of him, who fawned on him and flattered him continuously. He was used to obedience, to having his own way, and he was unused to opposition. It would have been natural if, urged on by his victory and driven by his ambition, he had ignored facts and advanced ahead.

But, realising his limitations, he decided to withdraw. He called his sheiks and headmen and advised them that the time was not yet: they had good loot enough to keep them comfortable for many months : a more convenient time would come later. He persuaded them to lead the men home. He called off the Ikhwan. His leadership was now unchallenged and they obeyed him.

Placing a garrison in Khurma and receiving the submission of the Ataiba he marched away into the Inner Desert, turning his back on the open road to Mecca, to the conquest of the Sacred Land and the renown which such a conquest would bring him.

As he went he realised that, though the Turks were gone, the English had taken their place and inherited their policies.

PART X

CHAPTER LI

IBN SAUD had drawn off, but he had not given up his ambitions. When the time came he would advance again, conquer the Hejaz and rule all Arabia. For the moment he had returned to Riad and would wait and watch. All round him was in a state of flux.

The Great War had smashed the Turkish Empire into pieces. As long as it existed, despite its rottenness and its feeble administration, nonetheless it had, by the prestige of age and of long-established government, held all the Middle East and the Arab countries together as one whole.

The Turks were gone. The ancient control and system had disappeared. The Turkish Empire had broken up into a debris of jarring, rough-edged, and undefined pieces—Syria, Palestine, the Hejaz, the Yemen, the Asir, Iraq, Egypt, Central Arabia.

For the moment they were kept together by the English. At the summit of their World Power, with immense prestige and vast military forces, the English held the Arab countries together as the cords of a net might hold a pile of broken pieces. They had garrisons in Cairo and Constantinople, in Baghdad, Aleppo, and Damascus, from the Red Sea to the Black Sea, and from the Balkans and Egypt to India and the Persian Gulf. The future of all the Arab countries was in their hands. Only in Central Arabia, in Nejd, they had no direct control.

But to continue to hold these vast lands indefinitely was impossible. It would require immense armies, and already the English soldiers, war-weary and without interest in the Arabs, were demanding to be demobilised and sent home; and the people of England were insisting that all foreign commitments should be reduced at once. They were not prepared to expend money or men on the Arabs.

To meet the situation the English Government devised a simple, clear-cut scheme. It was an adjustment of the ideas of the Syrian Revolutionary Committee and of Husein. They planned a Confederacy of Arab States held together by a common language and a common religion, ruled over by one head and controlled by themselves. This would require little money and few soldiers.

Husein, as Sherif of Mecca, should be the head of the Confederacy. They had already promised him this during the War. As Guardian of the Sacred Cities of Islam he still had much prestige among Moslems. They would make him Caliph of Islam. He would be useful in dealing with the Moslems in India. He would, they thought, be easy to control. His sons should rule the new states.

The scheme seemed simple and easy. It soon became complicated with difficulties. It was not based on realities. There was no national Arab feeling. None of the Arab countries wished to combine and certainly not under Husein. Each was split by internal dissensions. Two of the principal states, Syria and Palestine, had already been promised, Syria to the French and Palestine to the Jews as a national home. Husein claimed both and refused to agree to anything until his claim was satisfied. The French and the Jews were equally determined that the promises made to them should be fulfilled. The French, and the other Allies, resented the English control of the Arab countries and worked against the formation of the Confederacy.

Moreover, Husein and his family were not fit to play their roles. His eldest and youngest sons, Ali and Zaid, were poor creatures. Abdullah was an incapable, fat, blustering fellow. Feisal, the third and best, was pleasant in manner but weak in character, while Husein himself had neither the capacity or character nor position to carry out his part. Autocratic and obstinate he was disliked by his own people and despised by all moslems as the man who had, for his own glory and worldly advancement, betrayed his brother moslems, the Turks, and sold his own country to the English—the Arabs looked on the Turks, now they were defeated and gone, as their brother moslems and as martyrs. Husein and his sons might be bolstered up by the English : they could never stand alone.

The experts who advised the English Government increased the complications. Grouped round T. E. Lawrence they fought tooth and nail for Husein and his family.

Lawrence was the man who in 1916 had been sent from Egypt to save Husein's revolt from being crushed by the Turks. He had become the driving force of the Arab revolt and had led Husein's men to victory and to Damascus. His wartime exploits had given him great prestige in England. He was accepted as the expert on Arabia, and he led the English Government by the nose down the wrong path.

In Cairo, in London, at the Peace Conference in Paris, he demanded that the promises given to Husein should be kept while those given to the French and the Jews should be broken. His attitude encouraged Husein to be obstinate. He treated the French with such brutal candour—a candour with which he concealed much ignorance—that in negotiations with them he was as sand in the machinery, and the French became resentful and unyielding.

He was obsessed with the Arab Confederacy and could not see that it was unworkable. He did not know or he ignored the worthlessness of Husein. Of Arabia as a whole, of the Inner Desert, of the Wahabis and Ikhwan, and above all of Ibn Saud he was ignorant. St. John Philby, who had been the English delegate in Riad, knew the facts. Lawrence refused to listen to him, and he misjudged the strength and value of Ibn Saud.

For the English, Ibn Saud was no more than a tribal sheik

successful for the moment, who had appeared suddenly out of the desert with his murdering bedouin and his wild, fanatical Wahabis and Ikhwans. There was no place for him in their Arab Confederacy.

He was not of great importance they said—Turaba had been an unfortunate incident—but as a raider and a destroyer he interfered with their plans and he must be shut back into the desert. Their Confederacy of Arab States would form a ring round him and do that.

CHAPTER LII

AWAY in Riad, Ibn Saud heard of some of these things. He sent messengers to the French in Damascus for news and to get into touch with them. What he heard made him uneasy.

As soon as the Turks had gone the Rashid had placed himself under the protection of Husein. Now there was news that the English in Baghdad were considering an alliance with the Rashid against himself. That was the old Turkish method of playing one against the other. Salim, protected by the English, was working against him once more. Husein was boasting that the English had promised him help. With this he would recover Khurma, overrun Nejd, and revenge himself. The English had made Feisal King of Damascus and created a new State of Transjordania.

Ibn Saud called to the English to know whether they were still his friends. Late in 1920 he met Sir Percy Cox, who was the English High Commissioner in Baghdad, at Ojair; but he came away from the conference only half-satisfied.

Round him still, shutting him back into the desert, closing all ways out, was forming a ring of his enemies. Feisal, while Lawrence cried and threatened in impotent rage, had been ejected by the French from Damascus, but the English had made him King of Iraq. Abdullah they had accepted as Amir of Transjordania.

From Kuwait, where Salim was his enemy and English protected—to Basra and Baghdad—where Feisal was an English made king—across the desert by the country of the Rashid and his Shammar tribes to Transjordania—where Abdullah his enemy was Amir and English protected—down the Hejaz to Mecca and the frontier of Asir, there was a half-moon of his enemies supported by the English. With the sea-coast states, which were under English protection or alliance, there was a ring shutting him in every side, except in the Hasa.

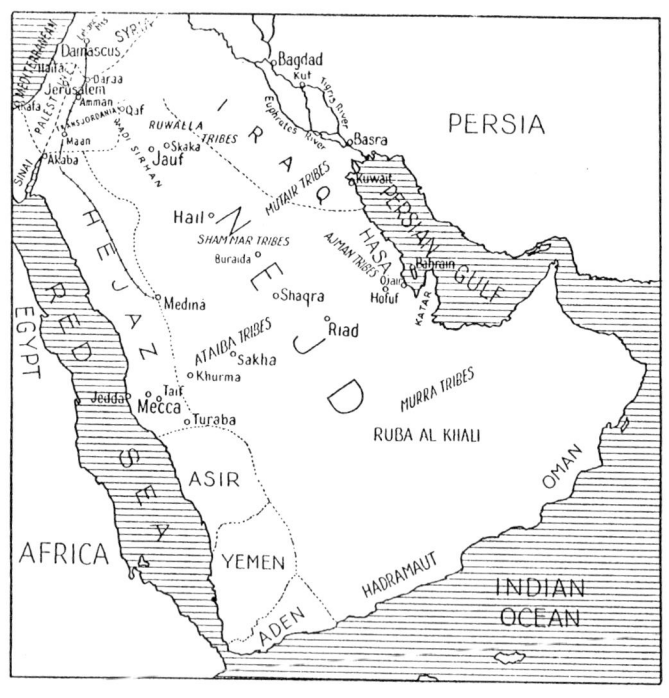

He would have struck at once and broken the ring of enemies, but wherever he turned he found the English supporting them, and he could not fight the English.

A lesser man might have lost his self-control and shown his animosity, but Ibn Saud held his hand, kept down his anger. He must bide his time.

He accepted the English subsidy as before. He remained courteous and friendly, but he watched and waited for his opportunity.

CHAPTER LIII

WHILE he waited, in the early summer of 1921, the opportunity came to him. The Rashid was the weak point in the ring round him. Ibn Saud had long since realised that and, as he had done with the Ataiba, he had sent out his preachers who had gone fearlessly up and down the Shammar tribes. The doctrines they taught, those of Abdul Wahab, touched something deep down in the hearts of all the desert people, and set them afire with a religious enthusiasm which destroyed all their normal loyalties to their sheiks and tribes. The preachers converted many of the Shammar, persuading them to forsake the Rashid and look to Ibn Saud. With this insidious propaganda—*siasa*, " diplomacy," he called it—Ibn Saud split the Shammar in their allegiance.

Moreover, the Shammar had no leader. The head of the Rashid family had been murdered that spring, and the rest were fighting among themselves for his place. They were powerless. Nuri Shalan, who was the sheik of Ruwalla, had sent men raiding down from Syria, who had taken the great oasis of Jauf which lay to the north of Hail. The Shammar had been unable to resist them. Ibn Saud saw that there was no strength left in the Rashid or the Shammar.

Everything was working in his favour. Salim of Kuwait, morose, ill-natured, cantankerous, hating Ibn Saud to the end, had died, and his successor Ahmed, wanted peace. Husein had promised the Shammar help, but he was tied by his own difficulties in the Hejaz where he had become more and more unpopular with his own people. Above all the English had their hands full. In Iraq there had been a fierce revolt against them. In Egypt, in India and in Turkey they were loaded down with troubles. Feisal of Baghdad without the English could do nothing. The time to strike had nearly come.

When Ibn Saud acted he did so with such explosive suddenness that often it seemed as if he was driven by the haphazard and unreasoning impulses of the bedouin. In reality he never acted without careful thought. He often hid his thoughts behind a mask of indecision, but behind that mask he pondered deliberately, considered the evidence, weighed the facts, and decided, but only with great caution. Caution was his outstanding characteristic in reaching a decision—such caution that often misled his enemies and even his friends into thinking that he could not make up his mind. Then suddenly he was convinced. He decided. He acted, with speed, ruthlessly, and without looking back.

So now he considered with caution, turning over in his mind and judging each factor, testing each step carefully before he took it. The Ikhwan were restless and demanding action. His advisers urged him to move, grew irritated at his indecision. Unmoved, unhurried, he kept steadily on his way until he saw the time and place best fitted to strike.

He sent out raiding parties towards Hail to test the position. They found little opposition and came back with good loot. Husein and Feisal warned the English of what was coming and appealed to them to hold Ibn Saud back. The English would have none of it: this was a quarrel between two rulers in the Inner Desert, they said, and no affair of theirs.

That was what Ibn Saud wanted to know.

The time to strike had come. He moved at top speed. He declared war. He sent Dawish with two thousand of the Ikhwan to hold the Shammar. He despatched his fast camel messengers to summon contingents from the Ikhwan, the villagers and the tribesmen.

They came in eager to fight. He received them, gave them their places in the march, in camp, and in the battle line, and divided out the camels between their fighting men.

As he prepared, news came to him one night that the Shammar had attacked Dawish who had beaten them back only with difficulty. Fahad, the Governor of Buraida, and many of his men had been killed in a cavalry charge.

There was no time to lose. He gave orders to break camp. In the grey light before dawn, after his slaves had struck his tent and he had prayed, he sat in the open transacting the last state affairs and giving final instructions. He was irritable. He chid those near him, flying into sudden angers, for now delay drove him to fury. He wanted to be up and off. The confusion of the camp as the slaves loaded the baggage annoyed him. Why did they take so long? Some of the tribes had not yet arrived. They were very dilatory. As the dawn showed all were ready waiting beside their camels. He gave the signal.

Mutrif of Riad, his standard bearer, rode out ahead and unfurled his green-and-white flag.

Behind Mutrif, all his irritation gone now that he was on the move, rode Ibn Saud, high up on his great yellow camel, towering above all. Beside him was his eldest son Saud, a youth of nineteen, and round him his guards, a thousand of the best fighting men of Nejd with their slaves, their camels swaying on the trot. On his right the Ikhwan in a solid mass and on his left the Dawasir in line. After him in line upon line came the townsmen, villagers and tribesmen, marching behind their headmen and sheiks, with their banners unfurled.

Ibn Saud had chosen his time well. The Shammar, without leaders, without co-ordination, honeycombed with disloyalty by the propaganda of the preachers, threatened in the back by Nuri Shalan's men, and without allies or help—Husein of Mecca had failed them: Feisal of Baghdad was a broken reed

—gave way everywhere. Across the grey granite country round Hail, Ibn Saud and his men swept up to the town itself, besieged it, and captured it.

Putting a garrison into Hail and sending his son forward with a detachment, he marched on through the Shammar country. Many of the tribesmen and villagers fled into Iraq where Feisal gave them protection—one day they might be useful. The rest submitted and swore fealty to Ibn Saud. Those he trusted he left under their own leaders. Over the rest he appointed his governors, but he dealt with them all generously. The males of the Rashid family he sent to Riad. He treated them well, gave them houses and slaves, but kept them as hostages under his eye. He married the widow of the murdered Rashid, adopted his children, and so linked himself to the family by blood.

In triumph he rode back. The people of Riad, led by his father, came out to welcome him: the Conqueror of their hereditary enemy; for many years no Saud had ruled in Hail.

In full Council, in the Great Audience Chamber of the Palace before the assembled leaders of the people, the ulema, the headmen and the sheiks with Abdur Rahman presiding, they proclaimed him Sultan of Nejd and its Dependencies. He was ruler of all Central Arabia.

PART XI

CHAPTER LIV

BEYOND Hail to the north stretched vast plains reaching to the frontiers of Palestine and Syria, where the Shammar and the Ruwalla tribes wandered as they grazed their flocks of camels and sheep.

In the middle of these plains, seven hundred miles to the north of Riad, stood the great oases of Jauf and Skaka. From them a long valley, the Wadi Sirhan, full of villages, ran another two hundred and fifty miles right up into Palestine itself.

Ibn Saud sent his men forward across these plains. His preachers had already been there and converted many of the tribesmen.

The Ikhwan, flushed and exultant with success, advanced. The Ruwalla were unable to resist them. They, too, were without a leader. Nuri Shalan their sheik had, in his youth, been a great fighter. As he grew old he preferred comfort to action. He had settled in Damascus where he lived at the expense of the French. As the Ikhwan advanced he did not come himself to lead the Ruwalla but sent a grandson who bolted back and after him incompetent subordinates.

Left in the lurch, first the Governor of Skaka and then of Jauf declared for Ibn Saud. One by one the villages followed. Farther north, up the Wadi Sirhan, the Ikhwan marched in triumph until they were within striking distance of Palestine itself.

The English woke to the danger. Jauf was the key to the northern deserts: it was a centre for the bedouin: it lay across the caravan routes from Egypt to Baghdad and from Syria to the Persian Gulf. Whoever held the Wadi Sirhan could threaten Syria, Palestine and Transjordania.

All the Inner Desert seemed on the move and about to burst out as the first Moslems had burst out thirteen hundred years before.

Dawish had raided into Iraq and beaten a force of the English-trained Iraq camel corps near Nasiriya. Some of the Dawasir were raiding into Kuwait and others into the Hejaz.

" Ibn Saud had upset all the balance of power in Arabia," said the English. He had become a menace. At any moment the Desert, at his orders, might explode and overwhelm the rich lands round its edges and destroy all their schemes of an Arab Confederacy. They sent messengers to him to halt his men and meet them in conference.

Ibn Saud might have ignored the English. His advisers were as excited as the Ikhwan over their successes. They urged him to push on : to march north to the Mediterranean, and eastwards to Baghdad : there was nothing to stop him, they said. The English were finished. They were being attacked by the Turks and the Afghans. India was about to revolt. In England itself there were revolts and upheavals.

But Ibn Saud kept cool and steady. He had a broader vision. He knew that the English were not finished. They were still strong. He halted his men. He sent delegates to talk with the English. As before he moved with caution testing each step before he took it.

As he negotiated, a body of Ikhwan of the Harb tribe, fifteen hundred strong, marched out of Shaqra at night and without his knowledge. Skirting Hail they rode fast northwards a thousand miles in the middle of August under the full violence of the summer sun with only their raiding rations. They crossed the Transjordania frontier and fifteen miles from Amman its capital, where Abdullah lived and where there was an English garrison, they raided a village of the Beni Shakir tribe, called Turaib. They destroyed the village and killed all the men, young and old alike, and such sheep and animals as they could not carry away.

This was a new form of warfare from the desert. The ancient rules and usages of tribal raiding laid down that only fighting men should be killed, and what could not be looted should be left. But the Ikhwan had no respect for tribal customs. They fought for Religion and the Glory of God. The people of Turaib did not conform to the rules of Abdul Wahab. They were heretics and must be wiped out.

As soon as the news was out the Beni Shakir attacked the Ikhwan. From Amman the English rushed out armoured-cars and from Jerusalem aeroplanes. They ripped into the Ikhwan. They slaughtered them wholesale, killing men and camels into heaps. Machine-guns and machinery, a torrent of lead, against men with rifles and swords. They chased them back across the plains. A thousand they killed and left their bodies to rot, food for the crows and the vultures, and examples to all raiders. The rest, without water or animals, were killed by the Beni Shakir who gave no quarter after they had seen the destruction of Turaib. Of the Ikhwan who started from Shaqra only eight returned.

CHAPTER LV

ONCE again the caution and judgment of Ibn Saud had been justified. He had recognised the realities. The Ikhwan had been blind to them.

News of the annihilation of the raiders of Turaib went out at once across the desert. For the first time the tribesmen had met modern methods of war. They had felt the might and the terror of modern man-killing machinery. They had learnt, too, that the English were strong.

No one realised these things better than Ibn Saud himself. The Turaib raiders had acted without his orders, damaged his success, and imperilled his position. In a fury he punished the town of Shaqra and the eight survivors of the raid.

Then, in the late autumn of 1922, he invited Sir Percy Cox to meet him at Ojair.

They were old friends these two, Cox and Ibn Saud, with a great liking for each other. Both were tall men, sinewy in mind and body, both were slow to decide and quick to act, both were shrewd and tenacious. Cox had an unlimited capacity for listening. He gave himself freely to those who talked to him, but he never gave himself away.

Ibn Saud talked much and eloquently, but when he appeared to be giving most he was in reality giving little. As he talked he concentrated on the man to whom he spoke as if he were his one interest in life. He had a smile, irresistible, all absorbing, which swept his listeners up with him, blinding their judgment so that each one went away satisfied and only later found that he had come away empty-handed; and even then did not resent the fact.

The problem to be decided between these two was a new one in Arabia—of fixing definite frontiers between Nejd and the surrounding ring of new states. Under the Turkish Empire frontiers had been unnecessary : a man might then have travelled two thousand miles from Aleppo to Aden and crossed no frontiers.

Moreover, the tribes who wandered continually throughout the year in search of grass for their flocks, deciding the direction of their march by news of rain or heavy dew, had rights of drawing water at wells and of grazing over vast areas. They recognised no stiff lines which they might not cross without passports or signatures. By moving from one area to another they did not change their allegiance. They were a community, not a territorial unit. Frontier lines in the wide free desert were unknown.

Here were two diametrically opposed ideas. The idea on the one hand of a territorial state with fixed boundaries and a fixed population, as in Europe, and, on the other hand, that of a loose, moving, undefined, nomad community. Cox wished to establish the fixed frontiers. Ibn Saud, realising that such frontiers would be unreal and that his tribesmen would never recognise them, endeavoured to postpone any final decisions. He had no misconception what it meant for him. He said to one as he waited for Cox on the seashore at Ojair :

" The English are my debtors, but I make no claim. And yet see what they have done to me—to Ibn Saud, their friend and ally. They spin and spin "—making a graphic twirling movement with the fingers of one hand—" they spin nets for me. They have surrounded me with enemies—set up states which they are supporting against me. The grey-haired one Husein in Mecca, his son Abdullah in Transjordania, his son Feisal in

Iraq. . . . Ever since Feisal came to Iraq the frontier troubles have not ceased. . . . And what is Ibn Saud, the friend of the English, in the eye of the grey-haired one and his sons? He is a ruffian, an infidel, a bandit. They have said all that. They have said more than that. They have persuaded the English of these things. They would shut me in."

The theory of the form of states did not interest him, but he realised that if he agreed to the fixed frontiers he agreed to the new states ruled by his enemies. He would deliberately have shut himself in within these fixed frontiers. He was determined to avoid doing that.

After many days of conference the two came to some agreement. Ibn Saud was recognised as the overlord of Hail, of the Shammar, and in Jauf. He should be paid a monthly subsidy in gold. In return he would recognise the frontier between Nejd and Iraq with the provisoes that there should be a neutral zone along it, that the tribes should retain their old rights of grazing and watering both sides of the frontier, and that no forts should be built near the wells or close to the frontier.

CHAPTER LVI

IBN SAUD came away from that conference dissatisfied. He had gained nothing. He had only strengthened the ring of hostile states round him. They were like a band round his forehead. His whole spirit passionately desired to burst the band but he had not the strength.

" See," he said to a friend, " when the English want anything they get it. We have to fight for what we need. I will put my seal "—punching the palm of his left hand with the knuckle of his right—" if the English say ' You must.' But I will strike when I can. Not in betrayal, God be my witness, but in self-defence. What I cede of my rights under force, I will, by the Grace of God, get back when I have sufficient force."

His whole instinct was to resist, to refuse to be bound ; but he recognised that he was up against superior force, that it was useless to kick against the pricks.

" We have to restrain ourselves," he said, with an angry roar, " and I have to keep my people in check—all the time. Let my enemies at least stop encroaching on me."

His tribes, especially the Mutair under Dawish, were as dissatisfied as he was. Not only were they to be shut in by frontiers, but they were threatened on every side and were forbidden to strike back. Feisal in Baghdad had armed those of the Shammar who had taken refuge with him and allowed them to raid into Nejd. Abdullah had sent troops into the Wadi Sirhan and seized some of the villages. Husein was threatening the Harb and the Ataiba.

The Ikhwan refused to be kept back any more. They retaliated on the Shammar by raiding in Iraq. They pushed northwards again up the Wadi Sirhan towards Transjordania and demanded to be led against Husein. In all directions the tribes were seething with anger, arming, pressing up to and raiding over the frontiers—and the heart of Ibn Saud was with them and not against them. There was big trouble ahead.

Again the English invited Ibn Saud to a conference, but it reached no result and only angered Ibn Saud, for Cox did not come and the English delegates did not know how to handle him. They treated him lightly. They did not realise that he was no longer merely the unimportant amir of the town of Riad but, that he was the Sultan of Nejd and the Lord of all Inner Arabia. They touched his pride and, like every Arab, once his pride was touched, he became cross-grained and unyielding, unmanageable.

"Yea," he said in a burst of anger, "I am friends of the English it is true, but I will walk with them only as far as my religion and honour will permit me"—and his religion, honour, and his pride had nearly reached their limit.

Still he kept his self-control, refused to bruise his head against the wall of the impossible, convinced that if he waited time would give him his opportunity.

CHAPTER LVII

HARDLY was the conference over before news came in that Husein had again advanced on Khurma and Turaba and taken both towns, while Abdullah and Feisal, to help their father, had sent bodies of men raiding from Transjordania and from Iraq into Nejd.

This was too much for the self-control of even Ibn Saud. Throughout all Nejd the tribesmen and the Ikhwan, even the townsmen, were up in a frenzy of anger, demanding revenge. Wise or unwise he would wait no more. He would attack Husein and teach him a lesson.

Suddenly he was taken ill with erysipelas in the face. He had from his father and mother inherited a tough constitution. Except for the one bout of rheumatic fever when a boy, he had never been seriously ill, but he had no reserve to fall back on in case of illness. He lived too hard, with constant work and severe physical and mental effort. He drove himself continuously and always at high pressure without any relaxation, flogging himself on even when tired. He neglected his meals and cut down his sleep so ruthlessly that the indigestion to which he was always prone had become chronic and a constant drain on his physical and nervous system.

The erysipelas became virulent and spread across his face. His whole system was poisoned. His temperature went up with leaps and bounds. He fought against it, refused to give in to it at first, but it was followed by further blood infections which laid him low for several weeks and reduced him to a skeleton.

He resented being ill. He resented being helpless and forced to lie idle. He would not let go for a little while and rest. He wanted to know all that happened, to keep his grip on everything, and he worried and tormented himself. He was a bad patient, often querulous and irritable.

When at last the fever left him and the poison was gone out of him and he had groped his way slowly back to strength, he took little care of himself. He began work before he was strong enough, and worked as hard as ever.

Four months later his left eye began to trouble him. He allowed the local doctors to treat him with quack medicines. The eye grew steadily worse until he could not see out of it. He called in a Syrian doctor who eased the infection but the eye was covered with a film. As this did not clear eventually he sent for a specialist from Egypt who operated and partially restored the sight.

CHAPTER LVIII

HIS illness had, however, stopped Ibn Saud from taking hasty and even unwise action, and while he lay ill events worked in his favour.

The people of Turaba and Khurma had risen against Husein and driven his men out of their towns and out of the neighbouring villages.

Husein had become very unpopular with his own people. Always obstinate, and if crossed or opposed ungracious, he had grown into a crazy and cantankerous despot. He would hear no complaints or appeals. He refused to deal direct with his people as before, which angered his Arabs, for it was contrary to all their ideas of government. They were prepared to obey loyally provided they had the right to criticise and complain. Husein allowed them neither. He was surrounded by subordinates who were dishonest and who filled their own pockets. He took it for granted that all who came near him were corrupt and treated them accordingly. He reduced the salaries of his officials on the supposition that they would make up the difference with bribes, which they did. He would listen to no criticism or even advice. If a counsellor dared to give unpleasant advice, he put him straight into the dungeon under his palace in Mecca.

He was rapidly ruining the Hejaz. The Pilgrimage was its main source of income. Husein had turned the Pilgrimage to his personal profit. He had taken control of the sales of sheep for sacrifice, of food and water and the contracts for transport of pilgrims from the ports to Mecca and Medina.

He forced the bedouin to sell their sheep and food to him

cheaply and he resold to the pilgrims at fantastic rates. He doled out the water only at high prices. He increased these prices in time of shortage so that many of the pilgrims, especially those from Java who were very poor, could not afford to buy and hundreds died of thirst.

He made high tariffs for transport which the pilgrims had to pay to him direct, but he paid very little to the caravan owners. When these protested he drove them away and in retaliation they took the pilgrims half the journey and then left them stranded in the naked desert. His profits he hoarded away like a miser or invested in property in Cairo and other cities abroad. He spent nothing in the Hejaz.

He had become extremely avaricious. Though Guardian of the Sacred Places and responsible, he cared not at all what happened to the pilgrims as long as he grew rich.

He neglected all the sanitary and medical arrangements so that great numbers of the pilgrims died of disease and neglect. He could not ensure security. His tribes raided and looted the pilgrims on all the roads. As soon as the pilgrims arrived they were set on, thieved from and cheated, and even forcibly enlisted into the army. In Mecca itself there were brawls and street fights, and Husein was too weak and inefficient to clear the roads of brigands or keep order in the city.

As a result of these conditions fewer pilgrims came each year and so less money came into the Hejaz. The English had stopped the subsidy they had given Husein in the War. To make up these losses he introduced new taxes both on the pilgrims and on the people of the Hejaz who resisted them. The tribesmen of the Harb and the Ataiba especially resented his impositions. A tax on each burial in Mecca caused a riot, and he was forced to withdraw it.

All the Hejaz groaned under Husein. Even his personal servants and his soldiers spoke bitterly against him for he treated them scurvily. They recalled the good old days when the Turks were in control; when the pilgrims came in their hundreds of thousands; when money was plentiful; when Medina and Mecca were tax-free and they were all prosperous. Under Husein the pilgrims were driven away and they, the people of the Hejaz, received no benefit, only loss.

Hated at home, Husein had made himself equally disliked abroad. He had isolated himself from all who might have helped him. He had fallen out with the Dutch Government over his treatment of their pilgrims. He had quarrelled with the Egyptians because they had dared to criticise him. He was on ill terms with the French in Syria, the Turks, and the Moslems of India.

He was still full of his big ideas. He was crazy with megalomania. He was "King of the Arab Countries." He believed that he was inspired from Heaven and he began to interpret passages of the Koran, and this became a scandal before all devout Moslems.

Sitting away in his palace in Mecca, surrounded only by flatterers, shut off from the truth, he was convinced that all Moslems looked to him as their head and that all Arabs wished him to rule them. As for Ibn Saud and such like, who would not submit, they were froward and stiff-necked and must be made to submit.

Above all he quarrelled with the English, his only real supporters. He demanded that they should carry out all the promises they had made to him, refuse the mandate of Iraq, and recognise him as the ruler of all Arabia: that they should turn the French out of Syria and the foreign Jews out of Palestine. He urged the Arabs in Palestine and Syria to resist and promised them help against the French and the English.

The English sent Lawrence to reason with the old man, to persuade him to compromise. They offered, provided he signed the Treaty of Versailles and so agreed to their adjustment of the Arab countries, to make a pact with him guaranteeing him protection against all aggressors—including Ibn Saud.

Lawrence, still misjudging the relative values of Husein and Ibn Saud, undertook the mission and did his best, but Husein would have nothing to do with him or the Treaty of Versailles and its arrangement for " mandates " over his Arab countries. The word " mandate " alone made him splutter with rage. He now wanted no promise of protection from the English: they would be asking for a " mandate " of the Hejaz next.

" I would rather," he said, " that the accursed Ibn Saud ruled Arabia than that it came under the foreign yoke of the English."

Again, late in 1923, the English tried to come to terms with him, but he was as obstinate as ever, and the English were by now only too glad to wash their hands of him. He had become intolerable in manner and impossible to deal with. He had lost all sense of reason or judgment.

The English were themselves in grave difficulties. In England the pulsing enthusiasm of war and victory had turned to lassitude and depression. Prosperity was gone and replaced by a slump. With demobilisation and lack of money they were reducing their outside commitments. They had many quarrels with the French and were not prepared to add another for Husein. Ireland was in revolt, a cancer eating at the heart of England and paralysing its energies. India was seething with sedition. The Afghans were on the warpath. There was trouble in Egypt, in the Sudan, in Iraq where the Kurds were up and the Turks threatening to attack across the northern frontier and seize Mosul.

In England, too, there was a general feeling that the strategy that had sent armies in the War to fight in the Arab countries had been wrong : that the campaigns in Iraq and Palestine had been a vast waste of men, money, and energy and had had no vital effect on winning the War : and that anyway it was time to cut all losses and get out of these countries and leave them to their own devices.

In the summer of 1923, seeing that Ibn Saud was preparing to attack Husein, Feisal went from Baghdad to visit his brother Abdullah in Transjordania. They tried to bring their father to reason : to persuade him to come to terms with the English and combine with them in some general scheme of defence, but the old man would not listen to them.

They appealed to the English to stop Ibn Saud, but the English were by now weary of Husein and his absurdities.

"Husein and Ibn Saud," they replied, "are both our allies. They are two independent rulers. If they disagree they must settle their own differences. We will not interfere."

As soon as he was well again Ibn Saud worked steadily against Husein, aggravating the animosity against him among his own people and isolating him from outside help. He sent his preachers among the disgruntled Harb and Ataiba and into the Hejaz itself stirring up the tribesmen. He kept in touch with the French. He was on friendly terms with the Egyptians and the Indian Moslems. He punished severely any of his men who raided into Iraq or Transjordania so that the English could have no cause of complaint against him. He prepared carefully on every side.

And Husein played direct into his hands. Early in 1924 he visited his son Abdullah in Transjordania. He treated that country as part of his own domains and Abdullah as his viceroy. He showed his resentment at the presence of the English officers supervising the administration.

Suddenly, without warning, on the third of March, the Turks abolished the Caliphate and ejected the Caliph from Constantinople. Three days later Husein had himself proclaimed Caliph of all Islam and informed the world of his new title.

The news raised a storm of indignation throughout all the Moslem countries and most of all in Arabia itself. The chance for which Ibn Saud had waited for so long and so patiently had at last come, as he had always believed it would come if he waited. He was ready to take it.

CHAPTER LIX

IBN SAUD had always been ambitious. From the days away back when, as a penniless refugee, as a rough, lanky bedouin boy, he had strutted and boasted before his companions in the streets of Kuwait and they had laughed at him—through all the years of fighting, in defeat as well as in success, he had never once lost belief in himself or in his people the Arabs. He believed that one day he would rule all Arabia, as his fore-fathers had ruled it before him, from sea-coast to sea-coast, from the Red Sea to the Persian Gulf and from the Indian Ocean to far in the north. All who had been the subjects of his ancestors would be his subjects.

In his success he never forgot the mission with which, he believed, God had entrusted him. He had created his Ikhwan as instruments to this end. Every success was a step nearer his goal. He was leading the Arabs out of that low state into which they had sunk, uniting them into one people, making them again into a Great Power and the Champions of Islam purified and revived. Already in many countries men looked to him as the creator of a new order and as a new leader against the imperial Christian Powers of Europe.

His enemies said that he had no deep convictions himself, but used religion for his own aggrandizement; and the fanaticism of his ignorant Wahabis and Ikhwan for his worldly ambitions. Even the ulema of Riad still suspected him of being too worldly, though they could not accuse him of laxness, for he was stricter even than before in all outward observances—the five daily prayers in the mosque, abstention from wine and tobacco, fasting, alms-giving, and studying the Koran.

In reality Ibn Saud was, by birth, upbringing, and conviction, deeply religious. He had a vivid, living consciousness of the presence of God. The strict training which his father had given him as a boy had fashioned the mould out of which came all his thoughts. Though not a recluse he was as devout as his father. God was for him a living personality ever behind his shoulder, when he was in public audience before his people or alone in the privacy of his own rooms, when he was in the heave and uproar of battle, or when he was sitting in conference—in the palace, in the open desert, in his tent on the march, beside him always guiding him, directing him in all his judgments and actions.

Before he considered any problem or difficulty he always first prayed in silence. As he came to the moment for decision, instinctively and automatically he hesitated for a space, made his mind void and empty, waiting for Divine Guidance.

His worldly ambition and his religion could not clash: they were one and the same. "I am," he said to one, "a Moslem first and an Arab afterwards, and always I am a Servant of God." God had called him to rule. All he did was for the Glory of God.

Despite all his enemies might say, Ibn Saud was no hypocrite. At heart he was as zealous and even as fanatical as his own preachers and Ikhwan. He had their supreme conviction in the sanctity of his beliefs and in his duty to spread those beliefs " by persuasion," he said on one occasion, " and if not by persuasion, then by the sword."

But his zeal and fanaticism were tempered by the practicable. He knew the practical value of fanaticism. "You should realise," he once said to Philby, speaking of his quarrel with Husein, " that I have but to give the word and a great host would flock to my banner from all parts. . . . And no one of them but is convinced that death is better than life, not one but lives to die for the great reward, and every one of them convinced that to turn back or hesitate is but to court the certainties of hell-fire."

He had the same belief and the same object as his Ikhwan, but in the means of reaching that object he was practical while they, blinded by fanaticism, would often rush into follies.

On one occasion Dawish demanded that he should declare a Holy War on the English. Ibn Saud refused: the Prophet, who had been himself the most practical of men, had laid it down that a Holy War, a *Jehad*, was only permissible if it had a reasonable chance of success. Success against the English was at that moment impossible: Dawish had himself seen what had happened to those who had raided Turaib.

Again the Wahabis in Riad urged him to have nothing to do with foreigners: such contacts were unclean. He refused. Foreigners were necessary to his schemes.

In matters of religion he submitted to the decision of the ulema, but when they gave him advice on political or military matters which was bad for the State he sent them back to their books. He would not allow them to advise him to the damage of his kingdom, which he held in trust from God.

He had, however, no illusion as to his mission. He did not set himself too high. Once there came to him a delegation which spoke to him of being Caliph, of taking up the task of the Mahdi and leading a Crusade against the Christians.

Ibn Saud heard them out. He was sitting on a high divan in his Audience Chamber in the Palace in Riad. For a while he was silent, his legs curled under him, his hands on his knees, his chin with its short stiff beard thrust forward and his eyes looking far away over the crowds waiting below him in the great hall. Suddenly he flung out a clenched hand and turned angrily on the delegation.

"With Mahdis and suchlike superstitions and sorceries," he said, "I will have no dealings. As to the Caliph, the question does not arise."

"I am," he continued raising his voice and repeating his

favourite phrase, "I am a simple preacher. My mission is to spread the Faith, if possible by persuasion and if not by persuasion then by the sword."

Both his ambition and his religion urged him to attack Husein: his ambition to expand his territory and break the ring of enemies of which Husein was the leader and the most virulent: his religion because Husein was not worthy to be Guardian of the Sacred Cities. He had allowed forbidden practices, smoking of tobacco, unauthorised prayers, prayers for the dead, decorations in the mosques, domes over tombs, luxuries and vices of all sorts inside Mecca itself. He had made the pilgrimage impossible for some and difficult for all by his malpractices.

Ibn Saud burned with zeal to eject this heretic Husein, to destroy the domes and monuments, to root out the unclean practices and the abominations, to purify the Sacred Land and the Sacred Cities, to make the pilgrimage safe for all and to enforce the precepts of Abdul Wahab who had expounded the Faith as it should be practised.

Beyond that he saw a vision—a vision when all the nations converted to the True Faith would form one great brotherhood, and when Mecca should be the centre of the world to which pilgrims would flock in their millions in eager devotion to do homage for the Glory of God.

CHAPTER LX

NOW at last Ibn Saud had his chance—the chance for which he had planned and waited—to be finished with his old enemy, Husein, and to conquer the Sacred Land and purify it.

But even now he moved slowly. He could not march straight into the Hejaz and conquer it as he had marched into the Hasa and as he had conquered Hail and the Shammar.

The Hejaz was a barren, empty land of rocks and sand, burnt to barrenness by a devastating sun. It was without natural wealth. It had little water, few towns and villages, and the bedouin tribesmen, who formed the bulk of the population, were ignorant and froward. Though it had harbours on the Red Sea it had no commerce, nor was it of any great strategical value.

But it was the spiritual centre of hundreds of millions of Moslems in all the countries of the world. Millions of these were subjects of foreign powers. It was for them the Sacred Land. In its capital, Mecca, had been born the Prophet Mohamed. Every Moslem hoped, before he died, to do at least once the pilgrimage to Mecca.

The Hejaz was not a simple Arab State, but international. All nations were interested in its administration. Whoever ruled the Hejaz would be an international personage.

Ibn Saud realised that, though he might take the Hejaz by force of arms, to hold it without the sympathy of all Islam would be useless. The Hejaz would then be a burden and not an asset. He must act with the consent of the Moslems of the world.

He worked on preparing his way steadily with his usual quiet, un-Arab persistency, unhurried and relentless.

He publicly warned Husein that he would never accept him as Caliph unless he was duly elected by all Islam. Then he summoned a conference of Wahabi and Ikhwan leaders to Riad. He needed the full support of his own people.

The conference was held in the covered courtyard of the house of his father, Abdur Rahman. It was crowded to overflowing with the ulema, the sheiks, and the headmen. In all the procedure Ibn Saud was careful that no one should be able to accuse him of thrusting himself forward unduly, as Husein had done.

Abdur Rahman, grown very old but still robust and alert, a simple, dignified old man with shrewd, wise eyes, presided. Beside him sat the ulema. Ibn Saud himself sat to one side without special position or honour.

One and all the sheiks and headmen voted to attack Husein. They spoke against him as the heretic usurper : for two years now no Wahabi had been able to do the Pilgrimage since he had shut Mecca against them. They were eager for action at once, especially the Ikhwan, who, as ever, were thirsting for a fight.

Ibn Saud took no direct part in the debate. Only when the Conference demanded immediate action did he intervene. He advised that they moved slowly. They would meet with much opposition from foreign countries : before they attacked the Sacred Cities they should obtain the sanction of their brother Moslems.

With his arguments the Wahabis had no sympathy. For them all good Moslems were Wahabis. The rest were *mushrekin*, worse than heretics. They, the Wahabis, were the only true Moslems and the only true Arabs. The only sanctions they needed were their own consciences. It required all Ibn Saud's personality and persuasive ability to keep them steady.

At his suggestion a message was sent from the Conference to Moslems in all countries detailing the sins of Husein, his maladministration of the Holy Places, his impositions, his injustices, and his tyrannies, how he had made the Pilgrimage a scandal and impossible for good Moslems, and how he had usurped the title of Caliph without sanction or right. And proposing that the people of Nejd, acting for all, should march into the Hejaz and depose Husein, as soon as the pilgrimage season was over.

The message was signed by Feisal, the second son of Ibn Saud. He himself did not appear in it.

It was characteristic of Ibn Saud that, even when he was advancing and until the final minute for action, he always left open some way of retreat; so that if he took the wrong road he could retrace his steps and reach his object by another. The Conference, and not he, should decide and send the message to all moslems. If there was an error it would be their error, and he would be free to put it right.

The message met with little response. Islam was split into a multitude of jarring sects. Each had its own differences in doctrine and practice. They hated each other, but one and all they hated the Wahabis more. They resented their haughty presumption that they were the only true Moslems. They remembered how a hundred years before Saud the Great had captured Mecca, thrown down the shrines and enforced the rigid rules of Abdul Wahab. They refused even to consider the Wahabis in control of the Sacred Cities.

The messages produced only a few replies, mostly vague, some in agreement; but the leaders of the sixty millions of Moslems in India sent their full and enthusiastic approval and named Ibn Saud as their champion.

CHAPTER LXI

ALL seemed ready for action. Husein was isolated. The English had repudiated him and even his sons had found him impossible to handle. His people hated him. The townspeople were angry at their losses and the tribesmen rebellious at his impositions. A great body of Moslems demanded his deposition and had named Ibn Saud as their champion. The Wahabis and the Ikhwan were up, straining at the leash to be let go.

Still Ibn Saud moved with caution, taking no risks. His counsellors, led by Hafiz Wahba, an Egyptian who had joined him many years before and who had a great knowledge of many countries so that Ibn Saud trusted much on his advice, urged him to attack at once, assuring him that he had complete victory in his hands; but he moved steadily on, unhurried, testing each move before he took decisive action.

Though he had kept his own counsel he had already mapped out his plan of campaign. He would attack through Khurma and Turaba straight at Mecca and Jedda and the heart of the Hejaz.

Now, partially as feints to draw off attention from his main attack, partially to prevent Abdullah and Feisal of Baghdad from sending help to their father, and partially to find out the general position, he sent out columns of Ikhwan—one towards the Iraq frontier, another across the railway between Medina and Damascus, and another from Jauf up the Wadi Sirhan towards Transjordania. He sent Sultan Ibn Bijad the sheik of the Ataiba, to raid up and down the Hejaz frontier and Luwai from Khurma to thrust cautiously forward towards Mecca and find out what opposition he might expect.

Beyond Khurma was the town of Taif. It was a pleasant place set among hills, full of gardens of flowers and trees and cool breezes. It had been protected with a fort and a garrison of soldiers and a high wall round it. The notables of Mecca had built themselves palaces in Taif, and here they and King Husein and his family came when the heat of the arid plains below had become intolerable.

Late one August evening news came to Luwai that Ali, the eldest son of Husein and the Commander of his army, had come to Taif for a change of air. Luwai sent word to Bijad.

Bijad, collecting as many men as he could, hurried down and attacked Taif at once. Ali, who was no soldier, bolted and the garrison of the town followed him. The townsfolk, left in the lurch, came to terms with Bijad and opened the gates of the town. As the Ikhwan marched in they were fired on from a police post and retaliated by massacring three hundred of the inhabitants and by looting many houses.

As soon as the news was out more Ikhwan flocked in from every side.

Meanwhile Ali had called up his troops and taken up a position at Hada, across the road from Taif to Mecca. The Ikhwan dashed straight at him, broke through his force, smashed it, and marched on Mecca itself.

CHAPTER LXII

IN Mecca there was panic. The massacres in Taif had grown in the telling until they had become a great slaughter. The people of Mecca, craven-hearted at all times, ran this way and that, wild eyed, slobbering lips, looking for somewhere to hide them and finding nowhere, crying out that the Ikhwan were on them: the Ikhwan were at the gates and would kill them all. Some took their goods and made away down to the sea-coast towns. The fear of the Ikhwan was a terror behind them. Ali, like his brother Abdulla, flying from Turaba, had rushed back to his father and increased the panic.

Husein bristled with pugnacious anger. The old man was no coward. He would fight the accursed Wahabis to the last. He refused to see Ali. He chased him out of the palace and out of Mecca telling him to be gone out of danger to the safety of Jedda. He sent a call out to his tribes. He summoned the people and prepared to resist.

But neither the people nor the tribesmen would come to his help. Even his soldiers and his servants began to leave him. Except for his household and his slaves he was almost alone.

He would none the less have resisted, but a delegation came to him begging him to abdicate in favour of his son Ali: as long as he was king they had no hope of negotiating with the enemy: if he abdicated they might get terms and save Mecca from assault: the road down to Jedda was still free of the enemy and he could escape to the sea while there yet was time.

Husein cursed the delegation roundly. He would not abdicate. He would fight. He cursed them for a pack of poor curs to be terrified at the first bit of danger. He drove them away.

Tawil, his Director of Customs in Jedda, the one man he trusted, called up over the long-distance telephone from Jedda and advised him to abdicate. Husein cursed him also. Tawil stopped advising and bluntly told Husein that it was his duty to his country. Husein flew into a passion and stamped up and down the palace like a madman.

His Turkish wife, the only person who could handle him when he was angry, and his family begged him to leave Mecca while there was time. Already crowds were collecting round the palace shouting that he must go: some were for killing him and taking the money he had hoarded: others for handing him over to the enemy in return for safety. They were threatening the doors. The guards were not to be trusted. At any moment the crowds might rush the palace.

At last Husein realised that he must go. He abdicated and prepared to leave.

In the palace were a dozen motor-cars. They were the only ones in the Hejaz, for Husein had allowed no one but himself to own a car. On to these he piled his worldly goods, rugs, bedding, gold and silver ornaments and boxes of gold pieces which he had received as his subsidy from the English. One car carried his family. Arming his slaves and the few soldiers still loyal to him he made them ride on the running boards, and at the head of this fleet he drove out through the streets which were full of hostile crowds who lowered at him but had not the courage to attack him—out from the city into the open country beyond and down the road across the hills to Jedda.

A week later Husein went aboard his private yacht which lay off in the harbour with his family and his goods, but especially with the boxes of gold pieces he had received as his subsidy from the English. He supervised the transport of those boxes himself. He counted them often. He tested the locks and the cording. He watched over them to be sure they were safe.

When all was ready he sailed away, first to Akaba and then to the island of Cyprus, to the end a pig-headed, irascible, preposterous old man, yet clean living and devout, without fear and also without common sense.

CHAPTER LXIII

NO one was more surprised at the complete success of his Ikhwan than Ibn Saud himself. Hafiz Wahba and his other advisers had foretold this success, but he had not believed them. He had never been quite sure that at the last minute the English would not step in and protect Husein. If that did not happen he knew that he could defeat him, but he expected at least some serious fighting. He had ordered Bijad and Luwai to go forward only to make a reconnaissance. He had not expected this sudden collapse of the enemy.

Even now with Husein gone the people of the Hejaz showed no spirit. Ali had returned to Mecca to organise resistance. He had failed, for the people of the town were cowed and the tribesmen would not come in. They were paralysed with fear of the Ikhwan.

Ali himself was a mild and good-natured little man, but no fighter. He had tried to stand loyally by his father, but Husein had treated him with contempt and refused to have anything to do with him. He had not wished to be king or to lead a forlorn hope. All he had wanted was to be left in peace, but Tawil had hustled him into acceptance and urged him to resist.

First he appealed to the English for help—a few aeroplanes, some money and arms, and their intervention against Ibn Saud—but the English replied that this was now a religious quarrel and in matters of religion it was against all their principles to intervene. They had at last realised the follies into which the misjudgment of Lawrence and the Arab Bureau in Cairo had led them—and the power of Ibn Saud.

Failing with the English, Ali turned to Ibn Saud himself and begged for an armistice to discuss terms of peace.

Ibn Saud refused bluntly. Until the whole brood of the family of Husein had gone out of the Hejaz, he said, there could be no peace; and he ordered Bijad and Luwai to lead their men forward but to see that they kept them in hand and that there were no more massacres and lootings as in Taif. He would hold the commanders responsible for any excesses committed by their men.

Ali, with the few men left to him and taking the police of Mecca, bolted and shut himself into Jedda where he had a strong wall round him and the English consul and the sea behind him if he wished to escape away.

Bijad made camp on the Nejd road outside Mecca and sent forward four of his Ikhwan on camels, unarmed and dressed as pilgrims.

They found Mecca silent, the shops and the bazaars closed, the houses shuttered and barred, for the people had barricaded themselves into their houses. Riding across the city through the deserted streets the four Ikhwan proclaimed that all were safe under the protection of God and Ibn Saud.

The next day Luwai with two thousand men, in pilgrim garb, but armed, marched in and took possession.

Luwai had nothing but contempt for the Meccans and their ways. Had he been free he would have treated them brutally, purged the city of their practices and forced them all, with the sword, to become Wahabis, but he was afraid to disobey Ibn Saud.

None the less, his men roughly manhandled the soft Meccans. They smashed the ornaments and decorations on the mosques, and threw down some of the tombs and shrines that seemed to them idolatrous. Beyond that Luwai allowed them no licence and kept them firmly in hand.

From Mecca they swept out over the country. The tribesmen and villages submitted without resistance. Only some of the tribes, the Billi and others named Wejh, in the far north, stood their ground; and the ports of Jedda and Yenbo with the town of Medina, which was strongly fortified, closed their gates and refused to surrender.

Except for these, Ibn Saud was the master of the Hejaz.

CHAPTER LXIV

AT once he summoned a great meeting in Riad and sent out word of his conquest to all countries. He announced that he had expelled Husein the Usurper: that he held the Sacred Land and the Sacred City, but he held it only as a trust for all: " Now that the rule of injustice and tyranny is over," he wrote, "our most cherished desire is that the Sacred Land of Islam be open to all Moslems and that the ordinance of the Sacred Places be decided by all Moslems. We ourselves will go to Mecca. We pray our Moslem brothers to send us representatives there to discuss with us."

Then, having appointed his eldest son, Saud, to act for him in Riad, he called his headmen and sheiks about him, the ulema and the notables, the captains of his soldiers and his ministers and, leading the way on his yellow camel, he rode out of Riad by the Meccan Gate, his bodyguard round him, and a great company of the Ikhwan marching behind him.

With this great host he travelled slowly making a triumphant progress across the plateau of Nejd, through the steppes beyond into the country of the Ataiba, and so up into the mountains of the Hejaz.

At each halt the villagers and tribesmen from far and near flocked in to do fealty to him and to rejoice at the news.

On the fourteenth day he sent his ministers forward with Hafiz Wahba his Chief Councillor and Damluji his Foreign Secretary to prepare for his arrival.

On the fifteenth day he passed through the last range of mountains that circle Mecca; and coming into a broad valley from where, laid out far below him, he could see the Sacred City, he dismounted and made camp.

Here he ceased to be the conqueror and became the pilgrim, on pilgrimage to the Sacred City. He put off his sword, his gold headropes, and his robes. He wrapped round him the pilgrim dress of two simple pieces of white seamless cloth, one piece round his loins and one piece over his shoulders, and with sandals on his feet, bare-headed, he rode on horse-back, unarmed and without pomp or ceremony, past the mountain of Arafat, by the valley of Abtah and the wide sandy road of Muabda, down to the Sacred City, repeating many times as he went the *talbiya*:

" Here am I, O God, at Thy command

. . . .

Thou art One and Alone. Here am I."

By the Graveyard of the Maala he was met by Luwai, and, passing into the city, he went on foot, with the Ikhwan and the people pressing round him, to the Great Mosque and there he performed all the rites of the lesser pilgrimage, of the *Umra*, with humble reverence as a devout Moslem.

PART XII

CHAPTER LXV

WHEN Ibn Saud entered Mecca he had made up his mind to maintain the Hejaz as the Sacred Land, as the Spiritual Home of All Islam, and as the centre of the Pilgrimage; and to increase its importance as part of his great design to spread the Faith and to re-establish the Empire of the Arabs, if God so willed it.

As to its administration and future government he was not clear. He needed the support of all Moslem countries. He was prepared to allow them a share in its administration. He had sent out invitations to them to come to Mecca and discuss its future. He had even said that he would leave its form of government and the nomination of its ruler in their hands.

Herein, however, he deluded himself. He was honest in his intentions, but eventually, whatever they had decided, neither his convictions nor his character would have allowed Ibn Saud to sanction anyone but the Wahabis to control the Sacred Places, nor anyone but himself to rule.

"We know ourselves," he once said to Ameen Rihani, a Syrian from the Lebanon who was cross-questioning him on this subject, "We know ourselves and we cannot accept the leadership of others."

He had not made up his mind on any definite line of action, and as ever he acted cautiously, feeling his steps forward, for he was on new and untried ground. Away in Riad he had sensed some of the difficulties ahead of him. There he ruled an isolated central Arab State of desert people. Here he was in control of a country with contacts that stretched across the whole world.

He moved, therefore, slowly, collecting and assessing the facts and then adjusting them into a policy rather than deciding on a fixed policy and forcing the facts, by lopping, pruning, or expanding, into that policy.

First he set up a temporary administration. The Hejaz was in a state of war. He declared a military occupation, appointed a Commission to rule under his general direction with his second son, Feisal, as president, and notables chosen both from Mecca and the rest of the Hejaz. He put Luwai in charge of the troops and made Hafiz Wahba Civil Governor of Mecca so that the liberal outlook and worldy wisdom of Wahba should balance the narrow fanaticism of Luwai and his Ikhwan. He sent troops to deal with the tribes in the north and to ring Jedda, Yenbo, and Medina round lightly with siege. He would deal with them later.

Hardly had he done this than the difficulties he had foreseen were on him. Whoever had ruled in Mecca had always been unpopular, whether it had been the Turks or Husein. Now it was the turn of Ibn Saud.

Moslem sects in many countries, and especially the Shiahs in Persia and Iraq, set up a roar of disapproval: it was monstrous and an outrage, they said with venom, that the Wahabis should hold the Sacred City: they were heretics: they would make the Pilgrimage impossible with their rigid fanaticism: they would, and had already, committed sacrilege as their fathers had done a hundred years before: they were savages. They quoted the massacres of Taif, the destruction of Turaib, the throwing down of the shrines and the desecration of the tombs in Mecca, and the atrocities of the ferocious Ikhwan to emphasize their remonstrance.

Ibn Saud sat quiet, listening to the uproar, handling each difficulty as it came with extraordinary skill—extraordinary because he had neither the training nor experience in handling foreign peoples. It was true that he had always taken a deep interest in international politics : that he cross-examined every traveller who came to Riad : that he had the Basra, Cairo, and Aleppo papers read to him daily : and that nothing gave him greater pleasure than to discuss foreign affairs. None the less, he was desert born and desert bred. Except for the few years as a growing youth in Kuwait, he had never been in close touch with the outside world. He had never been outside Arabia. He had lived all his life in the Inner Desert shut away, isolated, surrounded by self-centred and ignorant fanatics.

Yet with instinctive knowledge and much wisdom he handled the international complications that now came to him.

He showed no arrogance nor even irritation at the criticisms made by other nations. He invited them all to send delegates to the Hejaz to see for themselves.

The Persians came to see the damage done in Mecca. They were instinctively hostile. Ibn Saud won them over, showed them how little damage had been done, and sent them away satisfied.

The Egyptians who came were even more hostile and critical. Their hatred of the Wahabis was traditional from the days of Saud the Great and the Wahabi Empire. They were jealous, for they hoped to make Cairo into the capital of Islam and Fuad, King of Egypt, into Caliph. They complained—they had the information from Husein—that the Ikhwan under Dawish, who were besieging Medina, had bombarded the Tomb of the Prophet and destroyed the dome :˙ that Dawish had sworn he would loot Medina and massacre all its inhabitants.

Ibn Saud treated them with fair words. He showed them that the Tomb had not been bombarded and promised that neither Dawish nor his men should be allowed inside Medina.

Next came the Indians, more friendly but more difficult to

handle for they were wordy with democratic ideas and talk of western material progress, patter which they had picked up from the English. They were arrogant. They openly showed how they despised the Arabs and believed in their own superiority. Only by much tact was Ibn Saud able to side-track a dozen quarrels between them and the Wahabis, and even with the Hejazis, and send them home without open disagreement.

The Sheik of the Senussi came from Turkey. He was a devout old man with a great reputation and venerated as a saint. He had many followers both in the Hejaz and other countries. In accordance with his usual practice he made a visit to the tombs of the wives of the Prophet, and was said to have prayed that they would intercede with him before God.

At this the Wahabis were scandalised. No one, not even Mohamed himself, could intercede for another before God, they said. The Sheik had committed a great sin.

The Sheik retaliated criticising many of the Wahabi practices. A great quarrel began. Tempers began to rise. There would have been the final scandal of riot or murder in Mecca itself if Ibn Saud had not intervened and quieted both sides.

Thus from inside as well as from out Ibn Saud was beset with difficulties, disagreements, criticisms, jealousies, in one great hubbub, but he remained quiet and patient, and showed no irritation. Often he was so reasonable that his enemies thought he was being apologetic and sensed some weakness, whereas he was only feinting and testing them.

He was watching, learning the facts and planning his line of action.

CHAPTER LXVI

IN the middle of all these troubles and difficulties came an English delegation headed by Sir Gilbert Clayton.

The collapse of Husein had taken the English by surprise. They had expected a long war ending in some sort of compromise which would have left both Husein and Ibn Saud weaker and more amenable.

With Husein gone, they realised that they must act quickly and come to terms with Ibn Saud before he became too strong and perhaps too arrogant and stiff-necked.

First they annexed a piece of territory round the town of Akaba in the extreme north of the Hejaz. This covered the road across Sinai to Suez and Egypt and protected Transjordania on that side. Then they sent Clayton to see Ibn Saud.

Ibn Saud had made his war-camp in a valley beyond the village of Bahra on the road between Mecca and Jedda. Here he received Sir Gilbert Clayton, and his mission.

They sat down to talk in the mouth of his reception tent with a crowd of sheiks and Wahabis squatted round them listening. All round them was the tumult and bustle of the camp, the shouting and hurrying of men, the dust of horses and the roaring and grumbling of camels. Fresh bodies of men and new tribes came continuously marching in to join the army. Ibn Saud received their leaders, accepted their loyalty and detailed them places in the camp. Men with quarrels, complaint, cases for urgent decision, messengers came before him. He listened, decided, gave quick orders which his guards hurried to carry out. The interruptions did not disturb him. He came back after each to his conversation with the Englishmen without hesitation and without breaking the trend of the argument.

Akaba was not the important matter for which Clayton had come. Ibn Saud had quietly pushed his troops farther north beyond the Wadi Sirhan so that he held a corridor of territory

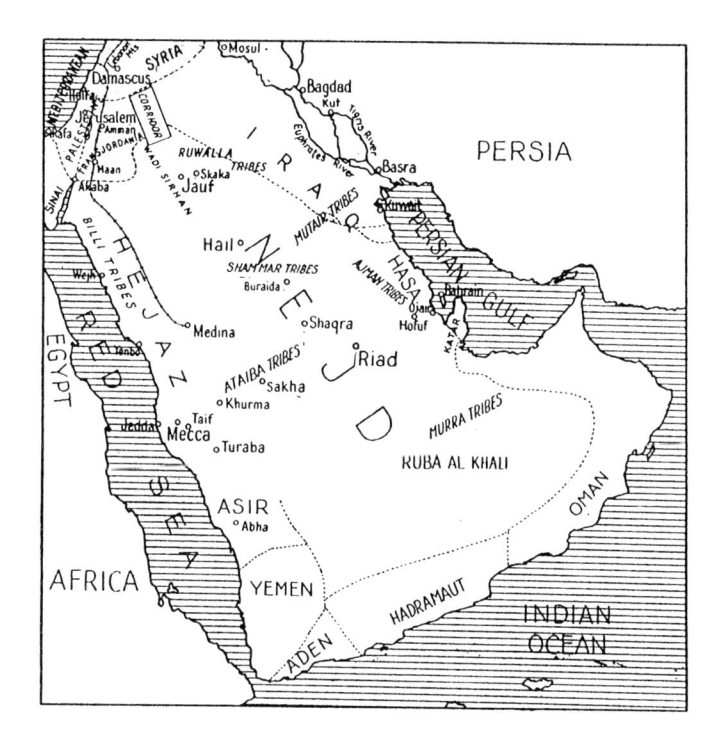

which reached up between Transjordania and Iraq separating them and which came right up to the French frontier in Syria.

That corridor nullified the whole of the English plans for the Arab countries. It cut through the ring of states they had made to shut Ibn Saud in, and it left him a way to break out to the Mediterranean. It threatened Palestine. It lay across all the routes for motor-cars and aeroplanes which they planned to connect up with Baghdad and so with India, and also the pipe-line which was to bring oil from Mosul to the English fleet which was building a new base at Haifa in Palestine.

Ibn Saud knew the value of that corridor. Pleasant always, breaking off now and again to deal with the urgent matters before him, he came back steadily to the same position : he would not give way : that territory was his.

Then Clayton played his trump-card. His orders were to persuade Ibn Saud at all costs. He suggested that the French had agreed with the English that the corridor must be evacuated by Ibn Saud and the frontier of Nejd pushed back. They had in fact signed an agreement by which they must both stand.

It was an ultimatum, a direct threat. For a second it stung Ibn Saud to indignation. He looked across to the camp teeming with men. He had only to give the word and they would one and all march against the English and march shouting.

He forced down his anger. He could not fight the English, especially with the French beside them. He had not the strength. At the moment he was weak. Jedda, Yenbo, and Medina still stood out against him. The tribes in the north were restless. Many of his men were tired and wished to go home. They had been many months away. He had much to do, to settle and to consolidate. He could not fight new enemies. He needed the friendship and help of the English to restrain Feisal of Baghdad and his brother Abdullah who were preparing to attack him and Husein who was sending them money and arms.

With a smile he turned to Clayton. He gave way. He agreed to withdraw from the corridor, to allow his enemies Feisal and Abdullah to join their countries and shut him back. Akaba he left an open question. In return the English accepted him as overlord of the Wadi Sirhan and the Ruwalla tribes.

CHAPTER LXVII

OFTEN with Ibn Saud, when he had grown sluggish with cautious calculating, a burst of anger acted on him as a mental tonic and stimulated him to make decisions. So now, after months of consideration, his anger with the English goaded him to decide on a definite line of action : he would hesitate no more : he would not let them catch him again in so weak a position : he would finish off the conquest of the Hejaz, eject Ali, and himself take complete control of the whole country as its ruler and king.

He had wished all Moslems to unite and, as one body, to consult with him in the administration of the Hejaz, but they had failed him. It was nearly a year since he had issued invitations to all Moslem countries to send delegates to him in Mecca. He had repeated the invitations. Some countries had refused : others had prayed to be excused for the time being. The few delegates who had come, whether to confer with him or to criticise, had soon made it clear that even on the smallest point they could not arrive at a common decision. They had spent their time criticising, quarrelling, and splitting hairs with unending arguments over unreal differences.

Ibn Saud was neither a theologian nor even learned. All his schooling had been rough and ready, and his ideas were simple and practical. Unity in Islam was his great ideal. Disunity he looked on as one of the cardinal sins. He had been profoundly distressed by the disunity he had found. It was disunity that had ruined the Arabs and Moslems and brought them down from their proud empire to their present state of decadence.

"It is written in the Koran, 'Keep fast to the word of God and do not separate!'" he said in one public speech. "God graciously gave Islam and Unity to Moslems. When Moslems separated they were defeated and God empowered their enemies over them."

The jealousies and quarrels, the hair-splittings, the shilly-shallying had only angered him. He wished to get down to concrete realities. He would wait no more.

His own people were pressing him. The Wahabis had repeatedly objected that these foreign Moslems, many of whom were heretics and who had spent neither money nor blood to liberate the Hejaz from Husein, should have a say in its ruling. They had made it quite clear that they would not agree to hand over the control of the Sacred Places to anyone.

And Ibn Saud knew that if he went against them in this they would resist him. Even he would not be able to hold them. The ulema, the Wahabis, the Ikhwan, the most loyal of his people of Nejd would resist him, rise against him, revolt rather than agree to what they would consider sacrilege—to allow the foreign and misguided Moslems to rule the Sacred Land.

The Hejazis too had remonstrated at the attitude of the foreign delegates who treated them as inferiors—the Indians in particular who had put forward a proposal to make the Hejaz into an international republic and offered to send their men from India to keep order and to act as police and soldiers.

The suggestion had infuriated all the Arabs, whether Nejdis or Hejazis. Did the Indians, they said, consider themselves so superior that they would lord it over the Arabs.

"I would rather," said a Hejazi to one of the leaders of the Indian delegates, "I would rather that Ibn Saud's black slaves ruled over us—ay, and misruled us—than you Indians. Go to! Show us first that you can organise one cooking-shop in Bombay before you come here to teach us how to run our country."

Ibn Saud realised that he must himself, without further delay or hesitation, take full control and be king. So only could he bring peace and justice to the country and protect it against outside interference, especially interference by the great Christian Powers.

" Of one thing be assured," he said to a foreign visitor, " there shall be no outside control in all my lands. . . . I will by the Help of God maintain this land in independence."

" I have considered," he said, " and I see that none of the moslem peoples can guarantee the independence of the Hejaz. The Indians are under the English, the Syrians under the French, and so on. Thus if I give them control the foreign Christian nations will control the Sacred Cities through their subjects.

" I alone have conquered by God and my own right arm and the loyalty of my people. I alone can rule the Sacred Land as a free State of Islam. It is my right and duty to be King."

He issued another general message to all Moslems: " I do not desire," he said, " to make myself master of the Hejaz or to take dominion over it. The Hejaz is a trust placed in my hands," but he added, and herein he showed his new decision, " I shall hold it until the people of the country shall elect a ruler for themselves—a ruler who shall regard himself as the servant of the Moslem World." And he knew that even the most truculent Hejazi would not dare to propose anyone else but himself.

CHAPTER LXVIII

WITH his conscience clear, his duty decided on, and his mind made up Ibn Saud set to work.

Hitherto he had not pressed the siege of Medina, Yenbo, or Jedda. He had only ringed these towns round with a screen of men. Now he gave orders to concentrate on them and if necessary take them by storm.

Dawish had come to Mecca to perform the pilgrimage. He volunteered to go to Yenbo. Ibn Saud, however, ordered him to collect his men and return home, saying that he needed him no more.

Dawish after some remonstrance set off intending to go to Medina. On the way he attacked the open and defenceless village of Awali and killing wantonly, he sent back word to Ibn Saud boasting of his exploit, asking for more arms and offering to take Medina by storm.

Ibn Saud flew into a great rage. He sent Dawish an abrupt order, to be gone and gone at once or take the consequences: there was no need of his help at Medina: he had committed many excesses—the killing in Awali was another—and made the name of the Ikhwan a scandal in the face of all good Moslems: if he was not gone then and at once he would feel the vengeance of Ibn Saud.

Dawish went back into the Inner Desert to Artawiya, and quickly, but in a rage, muttering and defiant, inciting his men to refuse but afraid to disobey.

Ibn Saud sent his son Mohamed to Medina. The inhabitants who had sworn they would fight to the end against Dawish surrendered forthwith; and Yenbo did the same shortly afterwards.

In Jedda was Ali. He still called himself King of the Hejaz. He had with him the remnants of Husein's army, the police of Mecca, and all who had refused to submit to Ibn Saud. He had engaged some Syrian and Turkish officers, dug trenches, repaired the walls and put out barbed-wire entanglements round the town and bought two aeroplanes.

But he was neither a leader nor an organiser, and his subordinates were incompetent. The town and all its arrangements were in confusion. It was at all times crowded, and now it was packed with pilgrims who had not been able to get away and with refugees from all parts of the country who had fled before the advance of the Ikhwan. There was no water supply except for a few wells and what could be distilled from the sea. The country round was barren without a garden or tree or even a blade of grass, so that even if the garrison sallied out there was nothing for them to get. There was no money, so nothing could be bought from overseas.

Soon food and water ran out and famine came on the town, and with it disease of every sort. Shut in within the walls the people died by the hundred and there was nowhere to bury them: a multitude of beggars covered with sores, too weak even to crawl, died where they lay, and their bodies rotted in the streets: men and women, mad with thirst and skeletons from hunger, killed the scavenger dogs for food, and fought for offal to eat. Under the fierce sun the town stank as with the pestilence.

When the Ikhwan closed in and prepared to assault there was no fight left in Ali or his men. To save the town from looting, and on condition that Ikhwan were not allowed inside the gates, he agreed to abdicate and go.

Early in December of 1925 he went aboard an English ship which took him to Aden and then to his brother Feisal in Baghdad. The last of the family of Husein was gone.

Two weeks later, when all had been prepared for him, Ibn

Saud drove down in state from Mecca. At the Medina Gate he was met by the foreign consuls. With his ministers, his guards, and the consuls behind him, the people and his fighting men shouting applause, and his standard unfurled before him, he rode through the town to the Great House of Mohamed Nasim by the customs-square.

There he stayed awhile, appointed Damludji as his Governor, accepted the surrender of the townspeople and issued a proclamation that the whole Hejaz had submitted to him; and returned to Mecca.

As he neared Mecca the notables came out to meet him and to tell him that the people of the Hejaz had elected him as their King.

Ibn Saud had entered Jedda in full state as a conqueror, not only to impress the European consuls, but also as a symbol of his victory over the heretic and usurper, Husein, and of the liberation of the Hejaz. He accepted the Kingship of the Hejaz however, without ceremony. He would allow only the simplest formalities. No one should be able to accuse him of pride of power or love of ostentation. These were displeasing in the sight of God. They were contrary to the practices of Mohamed and the first Caliphs of Islam who, though they had conquered vast empires, lived humbly as simple men without pomp or magnificence.

By the gateway of the Bab-es-Safa in the Great Mosque there was a raised place. There, early in the morning of January 8, 1926, he went without announcement and in his everyday clothes. For a while he sat, his brown Arab cloak drawn round him, listening to a preacher. After which he sent for the notables. They came and one by one touched his hand in sign of submission and fealty. When they had all finished, he went into the Inner Court of the Great Mosque and prayed.

By now great crowds had collected. With his guards round

him he walked through the streets to the House of the Governor. There he appointed his son Feisal and a Commission to act on his behalf and held a reception open to all. Only he allowed the gunners in the fort called Jiyad, which stood on a hill outside the city, to fire a salute of a hundred and one guns in his honour; and for even this many of the strict Wahabis criticised him for worldly pride.

CHAPTER LXIX

IBN SAUD was the ruler of all the Hejaz and of Nejd; but he realised more and more that, though in Nejd he needed no outside help, in the Hejaz on the other hand, if it were to remain the centre of Islam, he must have the friendship and support of all Moslems. Once again he sent out invitations for a Congress in Mecca and this time, now that there was no doubt that he was master of the country, delegates came eagerly.

On June 6, 1926, they assembled in the main hall of the Turkish artillery barracks which stood on a hill of grey stone outside the west entrance of the city. There were some seventy delegates from most of the principal countries, though none came from Persia or Iraq and those from Turkey, the Yemen, Egypt and Afghanistan, arrived several days late.

Everything had been carefully arranged. The hall had been redecorated, with the shutters, curtains, and fittings in green, the colour of Nejd. At one end was a dais. Below it were two tables horse-shoe shaped so that the delegates could not cavil at the order of seniority in which they sat.

The sides of the road from the city to the barracks and the top of the bare hill had been covered with a layer of earth, sown with barley and kept watered so that the young shoots should make a pleasant relief to the eye from the dusty, burnt-up country round; for the fierce summer sun had parched up all the land.

As soon as the delegates had taken their places Ibn Saud, without ceremony, with Hafiz Wahba behind him, strode in and walked swiftly up the hall to the dais.

He welcomed the delegates and then sat down while Hafiz

Wahba read a speech which he had prepared and which ended, "I invite you to this assembly to discuss and explore every avenue for the moral and religious betterment of the Hejaz, which may be satisfactory to God and man alike." After that he went out quickly as he had come, bowing to the delegates and leaving them to debate without the restraint of his presence.

That speech left no doubt as to Ibn Saud's intentions. Had they come earlier when he had first invited them and before he was king it might have been different, but now he had made up his mind on his own position and duty and on the functions of the delegates. He needed their support but, even to gain that he would not allow them to interfere in the administration of the country. He was king and he would rule. He would listen to advice and suggestions, but he would decide. All questions of his own position, of politics, or the ruling of the Hejaz were for him alone.

At a later meeting a delegate asked him why he had taken it on him to be king.

"Can any of you," he asked, facing the assembled delegates with his chin thrust forward and his face set, "Can any of you guarantee the neutrality and integrity of this Sacred Land against foreign aggression?" and when no one replied: "Then it is my duty to be king. I alone can rule and maintain the Sacred Land as a free state of Islam."

The delegates were there to discuss the Pilgrimage and the religious administration. All civil administration was for him and him alone.

"We invite you," he said, "to examine all means whereby the Sacred Places may become the truest centres of Islamic culture, models of cleanliness and hygiene and so exemplary a land as shall ever make Islam rightly known and famed" It was for this that he had called them together. Beyond this he would not let them go.

Even in religious matters he would allow little interference.

The delegates proposed that they should organise the building of a railway from Jedda to Mecca. Ibn Saud accepted the suggestion gratefully, but replied that he would himself arrange it. They offered to collect large sums of money from their own countries and, on condition that all the funds of the Pilgrimage and the dues paid by pilgrims were handed over to them, they would spend all they collected in improving the Hejaz. Ibn Saud, who realised that most of this was mere talk, expressed his readiness to agree, but first let them produce the large sums of which they spoke and then he would discuss the finances of the Pilgrimage with them.

He had learned to expect jealousies and lack of unity among them As the Congress debated he lost all belief in their capacity for action or sound judgment.

Their meetings were often difficult and noisy. They wrangled about every sort of question, and though they passed resolutions they were mostly of little value. They quarrelled and snarled at each other.

The Indian delegates were at the bottom of most of the trouble. One proposed the Turkish delegate, who had come late, as president when there was already a Hejazi in the Chair. Another persisted in talking in Urdu or English when the Congress had decided that Arabic should be the only language, and refused to be shouted down. Both criticised the Wahabi practices, the handling of the finances of the Pilgrimage, the organisation of the Congress, and the suggestion to hold annual meetings. They demanded more votes than the delegates from Nejd because there were more Moslems in India than in Nejd. They created a general spirit of ill-will.

While the Congress was still sitting there was a serious quarrel that showed the spirit among the various Moslem communities and the need for Ibn Saud to retain full control.

The Pilgrimage that year was in mid-June. The pilgrims had

already begun to arrive and among them was the caravan of the Egyptians bringing the *mahmal* from Cairo.

The *mahmal* was a box-like erection with a tent-shaped top, and carried on a camel and which was escorted each year to Mecca by a company of Egyptian soldiers armed with rifles and with a field-gun. Originally the *mahmal*, six hundred years before, had been the riding-litter of Queen Shajarat-al-Dor of Egypt. In time it had become the banner and token of the Egyptian pilgrims.

For the Day of the Sermon it was customary to take the *mahmal* along the road through the valley of Abtah to the mountain of Arafat, passing through the village of Mina on the way.

The Egyptians, on this occasion, had reached Mina and halted as some of the party had straggled or fallen behind. The buglers sounded their bugles to call the attention of the stragglers as the crowds were very great.

The hills all round Mina were covered with tens of thousands of pilgrims. Among them were many Wahabis to whom all music was accursed.

Some of them crowded down to where the Egyptians had halted. One pointed to the *mahmal* saying that it was an idol and that the Egyptians were praying before their idol with music. Another saw an Egyptian smoking tobacco. Some began to throw stones at the *mahmal*. More joined them and became threatening. The officer in charge of the company ordered them away. They took no notice but continued to throw stones. He fired in the air. That had no effect. Whereupon he ordered his men to fire straight into the masses of men and women opposite them, both with their rifles and the field-gun, killing twenty-five of the crowd and forty horses and wounding a great number.

At once the cry went up and from every side came running and riding Nejdis and Ikhwan to the help of their brethren. The whole hill-side, the valley, the village of Mina were full of angry men with rifles in their hands, calling to each other and massing to attack the Egyptians.

Ibn Saud was in his tent pitched on some sloping ground outside Mina, when he heard the firing. He sent his son Feisal hotfoot for news. Feisal could do nothing with the angry tribesmen nor with the Egyptians. He sent a message back begging Ibn Saud to come himself and at once.

Ibn Saud came at once. Running quickly out of his tent, he leapt on to his horse which stood ready picketed, and shouting for his guards he came straight at full gallop into Mina. Already night was falling and the valley was full of shadow and clouds of dust. Laying about him with his riding cane, shouting to the Nejdis, he rode in between them and the Egyptians. The Nejdis recognising him even in the half-light as he towered above all those round him, drew off up the hillsides and waited.

Ibn Saud turned on the Egyptian officer.

" By what right," he asked, " did you take it on yourself to kill. There is in this land a law and a government. I am the ruler. Had you sent word to me I would have handled this."

"Out of respect of Your Majesty alone," replied the Egyptian swaggering " did I desist, otherwise I should have wiped out all this rabble."

With a great effort Ibn Saud restrained himself. His anger began to rise. This swaggering Egyptian was in his hand. He waited awhile gripping himself.

" This is no place for boasting," he said quietly at last. " This is Sacred Ground on which, as it is written, ' no man may be killed.' You are our guests. You have our protection, else you should have paid the penalty."

Setting guards between the Ikhwan and the Egyptians so that there should be no more quarrel, and leaving his son Feisal and Hafiz Wahba in charge he rode slowly back to his tent.

The Egyptian Government refused to give satisfaction. Ibn Saud stood firm. He was the Ruler. The maintenance of order was his prerogative. He would allow no man to usurp his authority or to encroach on his sovereign power.

The Congress, with little of value done and as full of jealousies and disagreements as when it started, came to an end.

The delegates went home empty-handed, but they had learnt that Ibn Saud was, and meant to remain, ruler and master in his own land.

CHAPTER LXX

TO the south of the Hejaz on the Red Sea Coast was the country of the Asir, and, beyond that, the Yemen. Over the Yemen ruled the Imam Yaha.

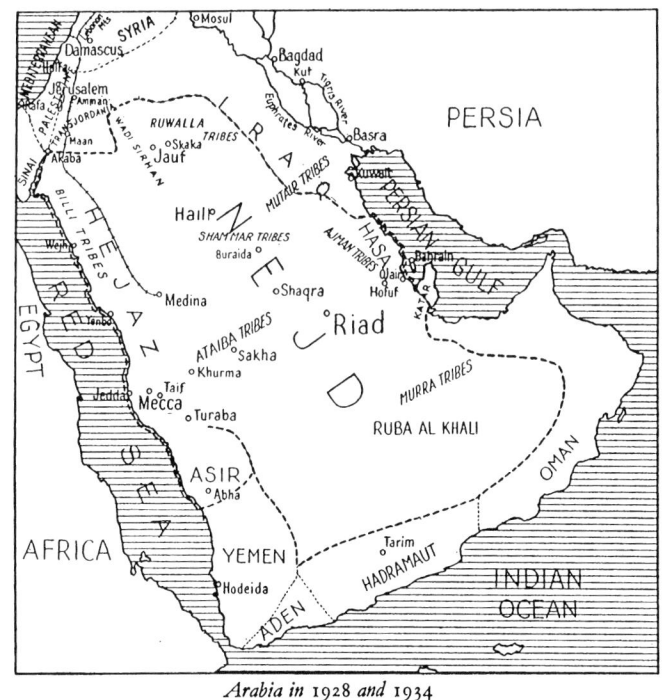

Arabia in 1928 *and* 1934
(*Heavily dotted line represents frontier of King Ibn Saud*).

The Imam Yaha was a strong-willed, despotic old man and he hated the Wahabis. The Yemen was a land of mountains but fertile, for each year it was watered by the monsoon rains driven up from the Indian Ocean and caught in the mountains. The people were sturdy and brave hill-men.

The Asir on the other hand was poor. It was torn with internal feuds. Up to 1918 the Turks had kept a garrison in the Asir. At the Armistice they had evacuated, and Ibn Saud had promptly annexed the eastern half of the country down to the town of Abba. The rest had for a time been ruled by one Mohamed Idrissi, but when he died and his heir Hasan Idrissi, who was both weak and unpopular, took his place, the Imam Yaha began to advance into Asir from the south and Ibn Saud from the north.

Late in 1926 the people of Asir had to decide between the Imam Yaha and Ibn Saud and they placed themselves under the protection of Ibn Saud.

Neither the Imam Yaha nor Ibn Saud wanted, at that moment, to fight. They came to an agreement that the Imam Yaha should keep what he held, but the rest of Asir should remain under the protection of Ibn Saud.

In reality Ibn Saud was in no position to fight. He had not completed the settlement of the Hejaz, and in Nejd there was trouble. His father and his advisers had sent him messages to come back to Riad as soon as possible : he had been away two years : too long : there was a general restlessness throughout the tribes : a feeling that he was neglecting Nejd for the Hejaz : Dawish was working against him : Hithlain was in touch with Dawish and rousing the Ajman : Feisal of Baghdad, with Ali his brother, was at work among the border tribes : there were many stories out among the Ikhwan of Ibn Saud's dealings with heretics and infidels : without his hand over them the tribesmen were getting turbulent : it would be wise if he returned and gave an account of his stewardship.

As soon as he had agreed with the Imam Yaha, Ibn Saud set out across the desert to Riad. His father and his son Saud had called a meeting of all the tribes and clans to greet him.

In the Audience Chamber in the Palace, the leaders of the people waited for Ibn Saud. They were prepared to cross-question and criticise him. They suspected that he had "allowed himself to be tempted by worldy interests into neglecting the interests of God." They were disgruntled and a little hostile. While they waited they murmured and muttered churlishly together.

When Ibn Saud strode in they were silent and rose. He went first to his father and paid him all respect. Then he turned and greeted the assembly.

At once, as he threw out a hand and spoke to them, commanding and welcoming them in one, the personality of the man asserted itself.

They forgot their doubts and their criticisms of him. They listened eagerly to his account of the conquest of the Hejaz, of the expulsion of Husein and Ali, and of the Pilgrimage. They grew enthusiastic, and at last they begged him to become also King of Nejd.

Ibn Saud accepted the honour. He was proclaimed King without ceremony—as when he became King of the Hejaz. He knew his people. He had won them over, but any show of worldly pomp and they would doubt him again.

Then making a tour of the country, receiving the tribesmen and the villagers and once more establishing his ascendancy by personal contact with his people—for the Desert Arabs had no respect for titles or ranks, for position or ceremony: the man and his personality alone counted with them—he returned to Mecca to complete his work there.

CHAPTER LXXI

THERE was much to do in the Hejaz. After years of misrule and fighting the country was without organisation and overrun with brigands and thieves. No road was safe for travellers and the people dared not venture alone out of their towns or villages. Pilgrims were robbed and killed by the hundred and without any action being taken to protect them. Murder was common, committed often for a few pence or a bag of bread.

Ibn Saud made security his first object. In Mecca he set up a police force of his bodyguard, for Ali had taken all the police of Mecca with him when he ran for Jedda. Into all the towns and villages he sent posts of Ikhwan and throughout the whole country camel patrols who moved rapidly, appearing suddenly in an encampment or village, usually moving by night and without warning.

The Ikhwan carried out the law in its extreme rigour, beheading for murder and violence, cutting off a hand or a foot for theft, and flogging for immorality or irreligious actions. Within the law they were merciless. They were tireless in their pursuit of criminals, never resting till they caught them. No appeals to mercy and no bribes of money moved them. They were without bowels of compassion. They had no respect for persons. There were no exceptions among them: all were equally relentless. They neither relaxed nor forgave, and in a very short time they had struck such terror in all ill-doers and enforced such security as had not been known in the land since the memory of man.

Serious crime disappeared. The caravan routes became safe

even for single travellers. The police-forts that Husein had built were evacuated as unnecessary. A man might leave his goods by the open roadside and return in a week and find them safe : passers-by would have made a detour round so as not to touch them even by accident. Two Ikhwan were sufficient to overawe a whole town or district; and the hand of Ibn Saud was felt from end to end of the Hejaz.

Next he improved the conditions for the Pilgrimage. Many of the tribes, especially the Harb, had the rights to levy dues on the pilgrims. These rights he annulled together with the rest of the exactions which Husein had introduced. He organised a system of transport from the ports to Mecca and Medina, fixing reasonable prices for the camel fares and also employing motor-cars. He arranged for the water-supply, and for doctors and hospitals ; so that the Pilgrimage of 1927 was crowded and more than a hundred thousand pilgrims attended in safety.

In Medina and Mecca he set up Committees of Good Morals whose duty it was to see that the people kept the streets clean, paved the broken roadways, repaired the drainage and lived decently and strictly by the rules of the Koran. Immorality of all kinds was severely punished, and luxury was discouraged : no man might wear silk or gold on his person, nor smoke tobacco. If any man failed to be present regularly in the mosque for prayer, the Committees must punish him.

Ibn Saud had already appointed his second son Feisal, with an Executive Council, to rule the Hejaz under him. Now he appointed councils in the five principal towns, Mecca, Medina, Jedda, Yenbo, and Taif, and in the districts, consisting partly of notables and partly of headmen chosen by the people, to advise him and to carry out his orders.

All government was as before concentrated in his own hands.

His rule was a personal rule. It was his personality, and not any machinery of government which he might create, that counted.

He worked as hard as ever, some eighteen hours each day, with little sleep or relaxation.

Mecca lay in a depression among volcanic mountains. Into it the sun beat down without relief until it became as fiery hot as a newly opened brick-kiln. After rain its air was heavy and languid, making all movement a burden. Its climate was unhealthy and did not agree with Ibn Saud. He travelled less, and worked more indoors. He had bought a motor-car and used it far more than he used his horses and camels so that he got little of the exercise to which he was accustomed. He continued to overdose himself with pills and emetics. He became more liverish and irascible. Yet though he was forty-seven, an age at which many Arabs have become old men, he was as vigorous and energetic as ever, and very little escaped him.

He hated red-tape formalities or aimless talk. He liked, once he had made up his mind, to give quick orders and be done with a thing, and yet in the greatest heat when all the world round gasped for breath he would spend hours persuading his men that he was right rather than give them orders when they were not convinced.

Nevertheless, he would stand no insubordination. On one occasion a number of Ikhwan had been detailed to go to Yenbo to take part in the seige. They appealed to Ibn Saud to be allowed to stay in Mecca as the Pilgrimage was about to begin. Ibn Saud heard their case and ordered them go. They began to murmur and complain and became truculent.

Suddenly Ibn Saud seized a sword from one of his guards, drew it and swung the blade aloft.

" By God," he said, "you shall go to Yenbo, and if I see any one of you here at the Pilgrimage I will slay him with this sword, as I slayed your fathers. Be gone ! "—and the Ikhwan went quickly without waiting or turning back, for they knew that he would do what he had said.

On another occasion when he was discussing with Clayton at Bahra, a party of the English delegates walked across ground where a body of desert Arabs were praying. The Arabs showed their resentment. Their sheik threatened the Englishmen saying that they had fouled holy ground by walking on a praying-place.

Ibn Saud sent for the sheik. " By what right," he said, " do you dare to speak in this manner to those whom I have chosen as my guests? And by what right have you holy ground reserved to you? O dog! all ground is of God and all is for prayer," and then and there, though the man was a sheik, he had him flogged for an example.

All rule was in his hands, and yet so vast had his kingdom grown that Ibn Saud needed ministers and officials capable of taking some of the burden of ruling off his shoulders, and in Arabia there were few to be found.

He took them wherever he found them, so long as they were Arabs and good Moslems. Abdullah al Fadl, the President of the Mecca Executive Council was a merchant of Jedda, and Abdullah al Suleiman, the Minister of Finance was a native of Anaiza in Nejd; but Hafiz Wahba, who had been many years with Ibn Saud as his Chief Councillor, was an Egyptian. Usuf Yasn, the Head of his Divan and his Personal Secretary was of Lattakia in North Syria and Fuad Hamza, who organised the Ministry of Foreign Affairs, was a Druse from the Lebanon in Southern Syria. Many of his junior officials were traders, merchants and schoolmasters from many countries, including Iraq and Turkey.

He relied also on his sons, especially on Saud who, since the death of Turki, had been his heir and on Feisal his second son. Saud had already shown himself to be a fighter and a ruler. He was much like Ibn Saud in build and character, very tall and strong, bold and direct in manner but more silent and reserved.

He had commanded one wing of the army under his father in

the capture of Hail. He had led the tribes in a dozen fights since then. In his father's absence he had ruled in Riad with skill. He was popular with the tribesmen, for he was generous and a typical man of Nejd in all his ways. He understood how to handle them and he was a strict and devout Wahabi.

CHAPTER LXXII

THE two countries which Ibn Saud now ruled, the Hejaz and Nejd, had little in common. For centuries the people had been enemies. They hated each other with ever increasing hatred.

The Nejdis looked on the Hejazis as evil-living heretics. The Hejazis on the Nejdis as wild, intolerant savages.

The Nejdis, shut away behind the desert, were rigid and fanatical puritans. The Hejazis with their outside contacts were more lax and more sophisticated.

Ibn Saud shrewdly used these differences. He established his Ministry of Foreign Affairs in Mecca and dealt with foreign countries from there, through the town of Jedda where the foreign consuls lived.

Geographically Mecca and Jedda were more convenient than Riad, but also he knew that the Nejdis resented all contacts with foreigners, and he foresaw that if foreign and western ideas worked their way uncontrolled into Nejd they would not improve but rather destroy the hardiness and fibre of his desert people.

New and foreign ideas he was prepared to adopt so long as they did not contravene the Koran, but many of such ideas were loaded with poison and he would himself be the filter through which they should pass to his people.

" There are," he said, " certain basic and hereditary characteristics which are the strength of my people. When new ideas appear I will test them—by the Koran. If they are not forbidden by Holy Writ, I will consider them ; and I, by the help of God, will judge if they be harmful for my people."

He would keep the people of Nejd from close contact with foreigners. This would be both to their best interests and in accordance with their wishes.

At the same time he was determined to utilise modern inventions. He had satisfied his own conscience that they were not forbidden.

" All my rule," he said to an inquirer, " is based on the Koran, and the Traditions of Mohamed. These do not forbid progress. They do not oppose machinery, wireless, or any normal developments."

He knew that if the great Arab Empire, which he visualised, was to stand four square on its own feet and resist its enemies it must adopt modern inventions.

" Moslems," he said in one speech, " are to-day awaking from sleep. They must take hold of the weapons which are at their hand and which are of two kinds—firstly, piety and obedience in humility to the commands of God; and secondly, such material weapons as aeroplanes and motor-cars."

But again he knew that his people of Nejd would resist the introduction of these foreign novelties. The Hejazis would accept them. Cautiously, referring often to the ulema in Riad for their advice and sanction, one by one he tried them out in the Hejaz—telegraphs, telephones, wireless, motor-cars, aeroplanes. But he had to work slowly. Often it took him months, cajoling and persuading, before he won over the suspicious Wahabis of Nejd.

Nevertheless, he never forgot that Nejd and Riad were the basis and source of all his strength. The Hejazis looked on him as a foreign conqueror: they were not loyal. The people of Nejd were his people, and Nejd was always his first thought.

He separated Nejd and the Hejaz and appointed Saud, his heir, as his Viceroy in Nejd.

In both countries all law and justice, all ideas, manners of life, even economics and taxes, were based on the Koran. When there were matters in doubt Ibn Saud referred them to the ulema of Riad, the Wahabi Doctors of the Law. In many sects of Islam there were ulema : he relied on the Wahabi ulema alone.

The ulema had much to say in the government. Ibn Saud needed them. He endeavoured always to rule by persuasion if he could. He knew that it was impossible to drive the desert Arabs against their wishes, but once convinced by a text from the Koran or a ruling of the ulema they would obey him willingly.

In all religious questions he deferred to them. They decided both for the Hejaz and Nejd—the sanctity of certain shrines in Mecca, the legality of domed tops to tombs in Mecca, the quarrel over the Egyptian *mahmal*, prayer formalities, even things that touched Ibn Saud personally. On one occasion one of the ulema criticised Ibn Saud in a public audience because his moustaches were too long. The Prophet had worn his close trimmed. Ibn Saud accepted the criticism. He would conform to the personal habits of the Prophet. He saw to it that his moustaches were cut.

In state affairs and in politics he asked their advice. Every Thursday, when he was in Riad, he met them in conference to discuss any question they might raise. Before he introduced the wireless, the telegraph and the telephone he asked for their opinion. Whenever there was any important difference of opinion between him and the tribesmen he obtained their support. But in state affairs he laid down limits for their interference and in all things the final word was his.

Thus with Feisal and a commission handling the Hejaz and Saud as his Viceroy in Nejd, Ibn Saud remained in supreme authority in both.

Meanwhile as he organised and strengthened his position the Russians sent an envoy to recognise him as " King of the Hejaz."

The English followed, sending Sir Gilbert Clayton to treat with him as " King of the Hejaz and of Nejd and its Dependencies."

After them came the French, the Germans, and the Dutch and many other countries; only the Egyptians hesitated, for they were still angry over the quarrel of the *mahmal*.

With the exception of the Yemen and the territory far to the south beyond the Great Waste on the coast of the Indian Ocean, Ibn Saud, holding a protectorate over Asir, ruled All Arabia from the Red Sea to the Persian Gulf and from the Great Waste to the edges of Syria. He was Guardian of the Sacred Cities of Islam and Imam of the Wahabis.

He was Lord of Arabia.

PART XIV

CHAPTER LXXIII

AT the moment of his success new and serious dangers threatened Ibn Saud. In all Central Arabia and especially in Nejd there was discontent among the tribes and this, while he was away in the Hejaz, increased unchecked.

Dawish had returned home from Medina to Artawiya with his Ikhwan and his Mutair tribesmen ; but angry and determined to be revenged for the insult Ibn Saud had put upon him.

He found many sympathisers. His Mutair were indignant that they had not been allowed to chastise and loot the heretics of Medina. Hithlain of the Ajman was an unrelenting enemy of Ibn Saud : he waited only to take revenge for his past defeats. Bijad, the sheik of the Ataiba tribes, was disgruntled. He disapproved of Ibn Saud's soft handling of the Hejazis. He would have treated them all as he had treated the people of Taif.

Dawish approached each in turn. He was related to both. His mother was an Ajman woman and he had married into the Ataiba. He invited Hithlain and Bijad to discuss with him in Artawiya, and there he worked up their indignation.

From Artawiya they sent Ibn Saud, who was then in Mecca, a letter of protest without mincing their words. He had become puffed up, they said, working for his own ambition. He was betraying the Faith. They had not ejected Husein to set up Ibn Saud for his own glory, but they had fought for the Glory of God alone. Yet Ibn Said had allowed the Meccans to go on in their old scandalous ways. He had protected them in their abominations. He had prevented Luwai from dealing with them. He had gone further, for he had himself introduced abominations, taxes on tobacco and on pilgrims, both of which were forbidden :

telegraphs, telephones, wireless and such like things that were witchcraft and of the Devil. They demanded that he enforced all the Wahabi rules in the Hejaz, and that he abolished the taxes and destroyed the foreign inventions.

Further, they called on him to declare the Jehad, the Holy War, on the people of Iraq, for they were heretics: their ruler Feisal was an instrument of the English: he sent his men raiding into Nejd attacking Nejd caravans and was not punished.

Ibn Saud hurried back to Riad. He realised his danger. If he mishandled his opponents they could raise half Arabia against him.

With Hithlain he knew he could come to no compromise: the feud between them was of too long standing and too bitter. Bijad was a stubborn, stiff-necked old man, stupid but all honest and devout, a fanatic. He would approach Bijad through the ulema.

Dawish was as stiff-necked and stubborn as Bijad, but, though he made a great show of his religion, he was not sincere. He was ambitious. He resented all restraint and control. He wished to be independent. He was driven by his personal hatred of Ibn Saud. He was astute and wily and he had far more ability than Bijad. It was Dawish who was the brains behind the opposition. Ibn Saud realised that he could not stamp on Dawish. He was too strong. He must work to isolate him and draw the tribesmen away from him.

He sent a soft answer back to the letter suggesting that all should be placed before an assembly of ulema for their decisions.

Dawish wanted no such assembly. He called Bijad and Hithlain once more to Artawiya and urged them to resist: Ibn Saud, he said, had agreed with the Iraqis: he would punish neither their heresy nor their raids: he was in alliance with the English to build a railway from Baghdad to Mecca which would destroy the freedom of the desert: and he had promised to give half Nejd to the English to be ruled over by them as they ruled in Baghdad.

Ibn Saud summoned Dawish to come to Riad and discuss before the ulema. Dawish came unwillingly, but not yet prepared to resist openly, bringing with him three hundred of his fighting-men.

Ibn Saud received him in the courtyard of the palace. Dawish came with his fighting-men behind him, their arms ready in their hands. Ibn Saud faced him alone.

Dawish was small, wiry in build, tough as leather and sour-faced. By nature he was turbulent and aggressive, but, as the Prophet had advised all Moslems to be humble in their speech and ways, he assumed an air of humility. This gave him an unnatural manner, as if he was for ever holding himself in, and now and again he would look up under his eyes to see what effect he was making on those round him. Because of this manner many men distrusted him.

Now he shed all humility. He was afraid of Ibn Saud and he would not show it before his men. He blustered. He was aggressive. He spoke in a loud voice and angrily. Again he accused Ibn Saud of betraying the Faith. He demanded that he should proclaim the Holy War on Iraq and that he should destroy the custom-houses and telephones, and all the foreign innovations he had set up.

Ibn Saud remained quiet, sitting with his hands on his knees, towering above Dawish, unperturbed, watching Dawish steadily. He knew he was in actual danger. Beyond Dawish squatted the Mutair in rows murmuring together and restless. A false move and they would be out of hand.

He spoke little and only in low tones and slowly. Gradually the bluster began to die out of Dawish. His aggressiveness ebbed away. He became quiet and tame. Ibn Saud was the master.

Then Ibn Saud called the ulema and bade Dawish and all the Ikhwan put their case before them.

The ulema decided that the taxes ought to be abolished and the Wahabi rules enforced in the Hejaz. As to the wireless and the telephones they were doubtful; it would be better if they were not used, but they were without sufficient knowledge to give a final judgment: as to the declaration of a Holy War that was at the discretion of Ibn Saud himself as the Imam: he must judge for himself.

Ibn Saud obeyed their decisions. He ordered the Wahabi rules to be enforced in the Hejaz and the wireless station which he had built outside Medina to be dismantled. But to declare a Holy War he refused.

Dawish persisted. He challenged Ibn Saud's right to refuse to declare the Holy War. He worked on through the tribes, urging Hithlain and Bijad to act without Ibn Saud.

But bit by bit, with subtle suggestions and shrewd propaganda, Ibn Saud jockeyed Dawish into a false position. He worked on those who already suspected him. Dawish had many personal enemies. Ibn Saud talked with his enemies. He drew a man away from here and another from there. He set the ulema against him. He persuaded them how at first Dawish had refused to come before them: how even when he had been given every chance to put his case before them he refused to obey their decisions. The ulema sent word to the preachers to warn the people against Dawish. It was clear that he was working, not for the Glory of God, but for his own worldly ambitions.

Some of the tribesmen began to suspect Dawish and ceased to support him. Even the Mutair split into parties, some for Dawish and some against him.

CHAPTER LXXIV

AS Ibn Saud worked and planned breaking the ground away from under the feet of Dawish and weaving a net round him to make him helpless, there came sudden trouble on the Iraq frontier where the Mutair lived.

By the treaty of Oqair Ibn Saud had agreed with Cox that there should be a frontier between Iraq and Nejd but that there should be a neutral zone on both sides of this frontier over which the tribes should keep all their ancient rights of grazing and drawing water; and within which no fortifications should be built.

Late in 1929 Feisal of Baghdad, with the consent of the English, sent a party of workmen with an escort of camel-police to the wells of Busaiya with orders to build a police-post as one of a line. Busaiya was the centre of a group of wells and was within the neutral zone.

The Mutair happened to be pasturing in that area, under one of the sons of Dawish. Already they were spoiling for a fight with the Iraqis. Now they saw their ancient rights threatened. They attacked, killed some of the workmen and soldiers and drove off the rest.

The English in Baghdad took up the quarrel, sent out aeroplanes and bombed the Mutair far out over the desert, within Nejd territory.

Dawish seized the chance. He sent one party of Mutair raiding into Kuwait as retaliation and himself made half a dozen raids in quick succession into Iraq, coming back each time with much loot. Each time he was chased by English aeroplanes which bombed his villages and encampments.

Ignoring Ibn Saud he sent out a general call for help to fight the Iraqis and the English and to take revenge for his dead. All across the desert the tribes answered and began to muster their men.

Waiting his opportunity and under cover of a storm of rain, Dawish with two thousand of his best men raided right into Iraq as far as the village of Jarishana which was close outside the port of Basra. He killed all men he met without pity. He destroyed the villages, cut down the palms, and left no living thing. Of the Jawasir tribe he killed three hundred men and carried off all the cattle.

After him came the English with their aeroplanes, searching for him and his men through the dust-storms and mirages which were as cloaks to hide the Mutair as they lay concealed among the vast sand-dunes of the desert. Twice they found and bombed them and then raided far into Nejd attacking villages and encampments as far as Artawiya.

Undaunted, Dawish sent a message into Kuwait that he would attack the town unless the port was opened free to him. The people of Kuwait manned their walls and called to the English for help. The English sent a cruiser to lie off the harbour. All along the Iraq border the tribes were in terror of Dawish. The Anaiza sent word that they would transfer their allegiance to Nejd unless Iraq could protect them, and the shepherd tribes refused to go south to look for grazing.

The Mutair were out. The Ajman were on the move. Bijad was ready with three thousand of his Ataiba.

CHAPTER LXXV

IBN SAUD was in Riad when they brought him news of Busaiya and the raids. He saw that unless he acted quickly all Nejd would be up in arms and out of his control. He must hold up the tribes or he would be rushed into war, and war with the English. Nothing would suit Dawish and his friends better. Nothing would be more disastrous for Nejd.

Most of the tribes were resentful that he refused to let them raid as of old. These would take the chance of war. Every malcontent and every raider would be out. The whole country would be again back in the confusion from which he had saved it.

He dispatched a protest to the English in Baghdad and called for an immediate conference. He sent out fast camel-messengers to the tribes, ordering some, persuading others to stand fast. Bijad was just about to move off. With difficulty Ibn Saud prevailed with him to hold his hand until he had talked with the English. Bijad agreed. Other tribes followed his lead. Dawish, thinking that his friends were failing him and afraid of being isolated by Ibn Saud, did the same, and to show his good faith even ordered the Mutair to hand back some of the sheep they had looted.

The English sent Sir Gilbert Clayton to Jedda. He came full of reproaches for the raids of Dawish. Ibn Saud regretted the raids: if Dawish were left to him, he said, he would deal with him: but he protested vehemently against the frequent and unpunished raiding of the Iraqis and the Shammar from Iraq into Nejd, the building of the police-post at Busaiya, and above all the raiding of the English aeroplanes across the frontier into his country while he was still at peace with the English. They had no right, he said, to take the law into their own hands. He warned Clayton that, though he had his people in hand for the minute, if the aeroplanes continued raiding the tribes would rise and attack Iraq even without him. The aeroplanes had been flying over Nejd territory, dropping pamphlets ordering the Mutair to retire four days from the frontier. This was ridiculous as the tribesmen could not read the pamphlets and it was unwise, for it weakened his authority and only infuriated his people.

All through the spring and early summmer of 1928, Ibn Saud and Clayton negotiated, but could come to no agreement. The Iraqis maintained their right and their intention to build police-posts. The English backed the Iraqis. Ibn Saud would not give way. Eventually he went to Mecca to perform the Pilgrimage, but also to show that he did not consider the position serious.

But the position was serious. The conference had failed. The Iraqis were being very provocative. They were full of threats. They were building more police-posts. The aeroplanes were again patrolling into Nejd. The tribes were once more becoming bellicose and unmanageable, demanding to be led to war against the heretics and the infidels who invaded Nejd. Bijad was preparing to move. Hithlain only waited the word from Dawish, and Dawish was at his old game. His messengers were going through the tribes telling them that Ibn Saud was in league with the English: he was weak-kneed and afraid of the Christians: they must act without him and fight to protect the Faith. Even the ulema began to talk of a Holy War.

Full of years Abdur Rahman had died and was buried in Riad. Very devout and respected, he had acted as a brake on the extreme fanatics and the most unreasonable of the ulema. They would listen to him when they would listen to no one else. His restraining influence was gone.

In the Hejaz too there was trouble. The Harb tribes had resented that Ibn Saud had annulled their ancient rights over the pilgrims. Husein had given them an annual subsidy to keep them quiet. Ibn Saud had stopped it. They had resisted. They had murdered a number of pilgrims and Ibn Saud had punished the tribe severely. Dawish had sent his messengers to them and they were again in ferment.

In the north, in Transjordania, Abdullah, fat blustering Abdullah, was breathing out fire and slaughter. He swore that he would chase Ibn Saud out of the Hejaz and restore his father Husein or be king himself. Working with Feisal from Baghdad he sent out his agents with money and promises. He worked on the Ruwalla and they became restless. The Billi tribes under their leader Rifada were out raiding round the town of Wejh, to the south of Akaba. Abdullah had promised them sanctuary if they should need it.

The people of the Hejaz too were regretting the lax days of Husein. Then they could make money by cheating the pilgrims, but Ibn Saud would not allow them to despoil the pilgrims. They hated the rigid unbending Wahabis. They worked underground, scheming and making plots and conspiracies. Ibn Saud stamped on the conspiracies. He issued orders forbidding political meetings and punishing any speech against the Wahabis and he chased sixteen of the ringleaders out of the country.

The Imam Yaha of the Yemen was threatening to advance again into the Asir He had newly made a treaty with the Italians who had come searching down the Red Sea looking for an empire and who hoped that the Yemen might be useful to them. This seemed his opportunity to force Ibn Saud to give up his protectorate.

But Ibn Saud's real danger was from the people of Nejd, from his own people. If they turned against him he was lost. He determined to meet the danger half-way. He dispatched a summons throughout the whole country to send him representatives to a great assembly in Riad.

CHAPTER LXXVI

IN the late autumn of 1928 the Great Assembly gathered in the court-yard of the palace in Riad. There came the ulema and the preachers, the amirs, the governors, the Princes of the House of Saud and the notables, the sheiks, the headmen, the leaders of the Ikhwan and the captains of the soldiers and with them many of the important tribesmen, townsmen, and villagers. They came in their thousands, and Ibn Saud faced them sitting on the steps of the palace while they squatted below him in row upon row, filling the immense court-yard from wall to wall and overflowing through the gateways into the public square beyond.

He knew that he must handle them with care. They had come with many complaints and criticisms against him. They had heard much against him. Many of them were hostile to him. This would be a test of his personal power and influence. Bijad, Hithlain, and Dawish had not come, which was an act of half-hearted defiance against him. Every man present knew that and was watching to see how he would deal with them. He would have to meet that defiance eventually. He had before him the representatives of all Nejd, of his own people. He must win them over to stand with him against his enemies.

It was an axiom of his " On one point I ask the advice of no man, for I know more than any man—and that is on the handling of the bedouin."

So now he showed his skill and his instinctive knowledge how to handle these men before him, both in the mass and as individuals. He greeted them as his subjects and as his brothers. He played shrewdly on their pride and their religious enthusiasms.

He treated them as the massed parliament of his people with the right to criticise him. He placed himself in their hands and asked for their opinions and their decisions. As long as they were allowed to criticise and argue with him they would afterwards obey him without hesitation.

"Might belongs to God alone," he said in his opening speech. "You will remember that when I came to you I found you divided amongst yourselves, killing and plundering each other. All those who handled your affairs, whether they were Arabs or foreigners, intrigued against you. They sowed dissentions amongst you so that you might become disunited and have no power or importance. When I came to you I was weak. I had no strength save in God, for I had no more than forty men with me, as you all know. Yet I have made you into one people and a great people.

"I did not call you here out of fear of any man. In time past I stood alone, and had no help save in God. I feared not for the armies of my enemies, for God gave me victory. It was in the fear of the Lord that I summoned you here to-day. It was the fear of the Lord and my fear lest I should fall into the sin of arrogance or vanity.

"I have heard that some of you harbour grievances against me and my viceroys and amirs. . . . I wish to know these grievances so that I may discharge my duty towards you and stand absolved in the sight of God.

"But first if there be any among you who have good cause against me, decide now amongst yourselves, whether you desire me to lead you or whether you will place another in my stead . . . I will not surrender my authority to anyone who would challenge me or who would wrest it from me by force, but I will surrender it into your hands of my own free will, for I have no wish to rule over a people who do not desire me to lead them.

"Behold, here in front of you are the members of my family. Choose one from amongst them. Whosoever you choose I will loyally support, and I will give you the pledge of God that whoever shall speak against me in this matter I will not punish him neither now nor in the future."

As he waited for some reply one and all the Assembly called back " We are all agreed. We desire none other but thee to lead us."

" Then," said Ibn Saud, " if there be any who has complaint against me personally, anyone who has a claim to make or a criticism to voice concerning me, whether it be on matters of this world or the next, let him speak out and I give him the pledge of God, His bond and His security that he is free to make any criticism that he wishes and that I will hold no blame against him; but that if his criticism is well founded I shall accept it and at once submit myself to the Law.

" Therefore, speak, O my people, and say that which is in your hearts. Relate what you have heard in criticism of your ruler or of his officials, for whom he is responsible.

" And you, O Ulema, speak, as you shall on the Day of Judgment in the Presence of God be called upon to give an account of your stewardship. Speak and fear no person small or great."

And the representatives spoke out of their hearts with candour and without restraint.

Every problem and grievance old and new was brought up and discussed; their mistrust of Ibn Saud's dealings with unbelievers; his friendship with the English; his innovations, motor-cars, and wireless; his lax handling of backsliders, especially in Mecca; his failure to stop the English aeroplanes from raiding into Nejd; and the raiding along the frontiers.

Ibn Saud kept them rigidly on these lines. He refused to let them discuss quarrels between one tribe and another or between individuals. These he would himself, as their ruler, judge at some more convenient time. They were there to discuss all difficulties between them and himself, and when that was done either to refuse him their allegiance or to give it to him whole-heartedly.

The discussions lasted for many days. Each problem was discussed backwards and forwards. Day by day Ibn Saud was present answering questions with steady patience, explaining, reasoning and when there was a point in doubt calling in the ulema to search the scriptures and give their opinions.

Outside the conference he entertained lavishly and gave many presents, as was his custom, to all his guests. He never rested. Every spare moment he spent in receiving the representatives either singly or in groups, talking with them, and making friends with them. Gradually he broke down the prejudice against his ideas and the suspicion against himself, which had been growing up in their minds during the last few years. So that when the Assembly came to an end, he had satisfied the vast majority of them, who went home converted into his enthusiastic supporters.

CHAPTER LXXVII

AS soon as Dawish learnt from his friends what had happened in the Assembly he realised that he must act quickly; very soon Ibn Saud would have him isolated and then he would strike him down.

He warned Bijad and Hithlain of what was coming. Early in 1929 they too agreed that the time had come. Ibn Mashur of the Ruwalla joined them.

Hithlain with his Ajman raided into Iraq attacking both Nejd and Iraqi villages on the way. Dawish with Bijad and Mashur called out their men to the number of five thousand, made to the north, demanded that the Nejd villagers paid taxes to them, summoned the other tribes to join them, and eventually attacked and looted a caravan of Nejdi townsmen who were coming by the main trade route from Hail to the Persian Gulf.

This was a direct challenge to Ibn Saud. Raiding over the frontier was disobedience to his orders which he would have dealt with gradually as the opportunity served. But this struck at the basis of all his authority—at his ability to maintain security and to protect his people. It was open rebellion and could not be ignored.

At once Ibn Saud sent out urgent messages calling up his levies. He must be quick and strike hard. If he hesitated or showed any sign of weakness every malcontent would be out raiding. He deposed Bijad, Dawish, and Hithlain and proclaimed them rebels. He sent Hafiz Wahba to come to terms with the English. They were ready to help him. They realised that, if he lost control, all the desert tribes would be up and raiding along the frontiers. They loaned him arms and promised to see that Kuwait, Iraq, and Transjordania gave no help to the rebels. He ordered Jiluwi to muster every man he could and attack the Ajman from the rear.

Men came in to him eagerly. The townsmen and villagers were solidly for him. They had long and bitterly complained that for years he had been lenient with Dawish and his Ikhwan; and they were ready to teach them a lesson.

The tribes, even the Ajman, the Mutair, and the Ataiba, were divided in their loyalty; some were for Dawish and the rebels; the majority were for Ibn Saud. Often even two brothers of one family joined opposite sides and fought fiercely against each other. Of the Ikhwan the most fanatical joined Dawish but the rest waited or were with Ibn Saud.

As soon as he had collected fifteen thousand men Ibn Saud divided his army into two and, putting his brother Abdullah in command of one and his son Saud in command of the other, he marched out of Riad and made his camp in front of Buraida.

For weeks the two sides manœuvred with raids and counter-raids up and down the country. Gradually Ibn Saud drove Dawish in. He cut him off from his wells and his villages so that he was short of food and water, and his men began to leave him, until at last in March he surrounded him at the village of Sibila near Artawiya. Here Dawish had made his base camp and dug himself in.

Ibn Saud sent in a messenger with a demand that he surrendered, and offering to leave all quarrels for the ulema to decide, but stipulated that Dawish himself with Bijad and Hithlain must stand their trial for treason.

Dawish refused. Ibn Saud repeated his offer and again Dawish refused.

Before dawn the next day Ibn Saud ordered Abdullah and Saud to close in and assault. Without firing, using only their swords, they rushed the camp with their men, and burst their way through the defence. Dawish's men fought back fiercely but they were outnumbered and within two hours the fight was over. Dawish was wounded and his eldest son was killed.

Ibn Saud had pitched his camp in a grove of palm-trees some two hours to the west of Sibila. He ordered Dawish to be brought to him there. When they told him that Dawish was come he strode swiftly out of his tent.

Dawish was laid out on a rough litter of planks and branches too weak to move from his wounds and loss of blood. Round him stood the principal men of Artawiya and his wives and children weeping, and a great circle of villagers and bedouin watching. He expected that Ibn Saud would order his immediate execution, but he looked up at him unafraid. His wives begged Ibn Saud for mercy.

For a while Ibn Saud, his face stern and angry, stood looking down at the old rebel. Then suddenly his anger died out of him. He bent down over the wounded man and forgave him. He ordered his men to carry him back to his house in Artawiya, and he sent Midhat Sheik al Ard, his private doctor, to tend him; and turning abruptly he strode back to his tent.

But it was not all generosity that made Ibn Saud forgive Dawish. Before God, the law and his people he had little justification for forgiving such open black rebellion. He had calculated shrewdly before he acted. He had first satisfied himself that Dawish was dying. He had staged the scene of forgiveness dramatically so that word of it should go through all the tribes. He had also proclaimed that any rebel who surrendered would be tried by the ulema. Bijad had not been in Sibila. He was away to the north with his men. Bijad was the real danger, for he was honest and he fought from conviction and not ambition, so that the tribesman trusted him and would follow him without question. Until Bijad was in his hands Ibn Saud could not be sure that he had broken the rebellion. If Bijad heard that he had been lenient with Dawish he might surrender.

His calculations were correct. Bijad came into the net prepared for him, surrendered, was tried and sentenced to imprisonment for life.

With the rest of the rebels Ibn Saud had no pity. He sent a force which chased Rifada out of Wejh across the frontier and slaughtered all who had helped him in the Hejaz. He sent Saud to deal with the Ajman, and his brother Abdullah to subdue the Mutair and the Ataiba. They burnt the villages and executed all the rebels they caught. They levelled many of the Ikhwan settlements with the ground and killed the men as a warning. Mashur hid. Hithlain took refuge across the Kuwait border, where, Ahmed the sheik of Kuwait, gave him sanctuary.

Satisfied that the revolt was over, in the late spring, Ibn Saud went to Mecca to perform the Pilgrimage.

CHAPTER LXXVIII

BUT the revolt was not finished. It simmered on underground. The Ikhwan were not intimidated. Dawish did not die. Tough in body and obstinate in will he recovered slowly from his wounds. He was not repentant but more bitter, and all that summer while Ibn Saud was in Mecca he worked rousing the tribes. He found the Mutair and the Ajman as ever ready for trouble. He sent word to the Ataiba to rise and release Bijad who was in the prison in Riad. He called to Mashur to bring in his Ruwalla. He spread the report that Feisal of Baghdad with the English were about to invade Nejd and had arranged that Abdullah should do the same from Transjordania, and that the people of the Hejaz would revolt. Ibn Saud, he said, was in league with the enemy : the people of Nejd must rise and defend themselves.

Jiluwi, hearing that Hithlain had come back and that the Ajman were preparing, sent his son Fahad to watch them. Fahad was a high-strung and unreliable young man. He invited Hithlain to visit him and gave him a safe conduct. Hithlain came with only five men. Fahad suspecting treachery killed Hithlain and his men when they were guests in his tents. At the news the Ajmen exploded. An Ajman shot Fahad in revenge. Even those of the Ajman who had not taken part in the last rebellion joined in. Jiluwi, when they told him of the death of his son, was so stricken with grief that for a time he was dangerously ill. The tribes of the Hasa without his strong hand over them became turbulent. Dawish with his Mutair and Ikhwan joined the Ajman.

Ibn Saud was in Mecca when he heard the news. He collected

every motor-car available and with two hundred he hurried back to Riad. As he went the Ataiba rose behind him cutting off the Hejaz from Nejd.

At once he sent Saud to replace Jiluwi and to hold the Ajman. He must play for time, for he had been caught unprepared, and he must collect men and get ready.

Again he sent Hafiz Wahba to arrange with the English to prevent any help or supplies going to the rebels from Iraq or Kuwait. The revolt was difficult to handle, for it was not organised as a whole under definite leaders, but scattered districts, far apart, would rise without warning, and in all directions.

Once again the stout-hearted solid townsmen and villagers of Nejd came out at his call together with many of the loyal Ikhwan and tribesmen, but this time Ibn Saud fought on new lines. He used his infantry, horsemen and camelmen in the traditional way of desert warfare, but he packed his best fighting men on to his motor-cars and moved them rapidly wherever they were wanted.

As usual the fighting consisted of raids mainly for wells and villages, but now Ibn Saud had greater mobility and quicker means of getting news than his enemies. Again and again he cut off Dawish's men when they thought they were safe. He caught detachments unprepared when they believed he was still fifty miles away. Hardly had a village declared against him before he was on it. He swept across the desert and arrested every stray bedouin so that Dawish could make use of no scouts and could get no information.

Dawish's men began to lose heart. They were not used to such warfare with machines. They began to desert. The Iraq frontier tribes took the chance to revenge themselves and attacked Dawish in the rear and looted his camps. The Ajman gave up and went home. Concentrating on the Ataiba, Ibn Saud smashed them section by section.

Still Dawish fought on doggedly. He knew that there would be no mercy for him. Twice he was wounded. A second of his sons was killed with seven hundred of his best men in one fight. As his men grew fewer he was chased up and down the country.

With Mashur and his remaining force he made for the Iraq frontier so as to have a way of escape open. In the Batin valley, where the frontier of Nejd, Iraq, and Kuwait join, they halted, believing themselves safe for the time being, but a detachment of Ibn Saud's men hearing where they were made a forced march with the use of cars, dashed into the camp, caught them unprepared and smashed them before they could resist.

Mashur escaped into Iraq, and got away to Syria where the French gave him protection. Dawish escaped into Kuwait, and surrendered to an English patrol which handed him back to Ibn Saud, who locked him into the prison in Riad with Bijad.

This time Ibn Saud saw to it himself that the rebels felt his anger. Without mercy, methodically and steadily he weeded out all the disloyal, burned their villages, harried their lands, and executed their leaders. On the disloyal Ikhwan he set his heel.

"Think not," he said in a general proclamation to them, "that we consider you of much value. Think not that you have rendered us much service and that we need you. Your real value, O Ikhwan, is in obedience to God and then to us. . . . And do not forget that there is not one amongst you whose father or brother or cousin we have not slain. It was by the sword that we conquered you. That same sword is even now over your heads. Beware, encroach not upon the rights of others. If you do, your value and the value of the dust shall be the same. We took you by the sword and we shall keep you in bounds by the sword."

The revolt was over. The leaders had all been dealt with. Hithlain was dead. Dawish and Bijad were safely locked in prison. Mashur was of little importance. Without leaders the tribesmen were like sheep. Both the tribesmen and the Ikhwan had learned their lesson. Ibn Saud was once more supreme and unchallenged.

CHAPTER LXXIX

ON one point the Ikhwan rebellions had decided Ibn Saud. He would retain all power concentrated in himself at the centre, but, to keep control of the vast empire he now ruled, he must have in his hands the best weapons with which to strike hard and quickly in every direction and to the farthest point. He must have motor-cars, telephones, telegraphs, wireless, and machinery of all sorts.

For six years he had deferred to the prejudices of the ulema and of the strict Wahabis. He had tried to persuade them that modern inventions were not accursed. Now he had made up his mind that these inventions were necessary for the safety of the State and he would have them without further delay.

He built a high-powered wireless station outside Mecca and another at Riad, and connected up the district with his palaces by wireless telegraph and telephone so that he could talk direct with his provincial governors and keep in personal touch with all that happened. He had four lorries fitted with Marconi sets which he used when he was travelling.

He bought motor-cars himself and he encouraged others to do the same. In 1926 there had been no more than a dozen cars in the whole country. By 1930 there were 1,500 running between Jedda and Mecca. All these could be commandeered when needed. In specially difficult country he built roads.

He reorganised his military forces. He created a small regular army. He had many of the men trained to use modern arms and to be technicians. He bought armoured-cars and four aeroplanes, to supplement six which he had captured from Husein. The Ikhwan were still his main fighting force. They could turn out fifty thousand fighting men. He made a drastic purge among them leaving only those he could trust, and he saw that they had the best arms. The levies from the towns, villages, and tribes he retained as before, but with wireless, telephones and motor-cars he could summon them more quickly and to the point where they would be needed.

He soon showed the results of his reorganisation. The Harb tribes south of Mecca revolted. He crushed them at once.

Ibn Rifada, the sheik of the Billi who had raided round Wejh during the Ikhwan revolt and then fled to Egypt, came back. Ibn Saud's enemies in Egypt, mainly exiles from the Hejaz, and Abdullah of Transjordania had given him arms and money. Raiding across the border from Transjordania he came southwards calling on the Billi to rise.

Ibn Saud had the news by telephone from his patrols almost at once. Within a few days he had ten thousand men concentrated in Taif and another six thousand at a point on the Hejaz railway. Controlling the whole force by wireless from Taif he used them to cut across Rifada's line of retreat. He caught him in a valley near the town of Dabha, killed him and his two sons and, with the exception of five men who escaped, he wiped out the whole force. Then he marched northwards and methodically cleared all the north of the Hejaz of malcontents right up to the frontier of Transjordania.

Hasan Idrissi of the Asir had decided to throw off Ibn Saud's protectorate and to make himself independent. Ibn Saud annexed the Asir. Hasan Idrissi continued to work for independence and revolted. Before he was well on the move Ibn Saud had the news, was up in the Asir, and had driven Hasan Idrissi back into the mountains, across the border into the Yemen.

About these actions there was nothing of the casual, desultory desert warfare of the past—news brought in weeks late by a runner or camel-rider, skirmishes with much dust and noise but few casualties, and often no definite result. They were swift, efficient, and as impersonal as the armoured-car and the machine-gun. They taught all the desert tribes what to expect.

On his frontiers Ibn Saud worked for peace. The ring of new states which the English had created round him had become only a half-moon consisting of Transjordania from the Red Sea and Iraq down to the Persian Gulf; but the half-moon effectively shut him in.

He had made up his mind not to quarrel with the English. He could not fight them. He knew his limitations and those of his country. He was on good terms with them. They had formally recognised him as an independent king and sent a a Minister Plenipotentiary to Jedda instead of a consul.

He came quickly to an agreement with Feisal of Baghdad to respect the frontier between them. With Abdullah of Transjordania it was more difficult, for Abdullah had taken up the family quarrel and swore he would not rest until he had chased Ibn Saud out of the Hejaz; and he had much of the obstinacy of his father Husein. He had been the mainspring behind Rifada. Eventually he too agreed to a treaty of friendship.

In the south alone there was danger. The Imam Yaha had taken the side of Hasan Idrissi and threatened to advance into Asir. Ibn Saud despatched troops and appointed his son Saud to command, but he opened negotiations which he continued month after month and postponed war, until the Imam Yaha came to terms.

Meanwhile, having at last some leisure from fighting he set to work to improve the condition of his people. He was handicapped by lack of money. The country was very poor, but made poorer by the world trade depression. Even the number of pilgrims to Mecca fell off, and those who came had little to spend.

Ibn Saud tried no dramatic or fundamental changes. He believed only in slow development. His people were ignorant, suspicious, and conservative. He tried to improve a few essentials.

In many villages he founded schools and he engaged a number of schoolmasters from Syria and Egypt. They taught Islam and the practical application of its teaching to life, adding a little secular and technical training.

Ibn Saud had no trust in purely secular education. All his ideas and thoughts were based on religion. " I have no other rule," he said, " nor way to follow save the True Religion, and the Sacred Book between my hands."

He founded a number of hospitals and set out travelling dispensaries and clinics among the tribes and villages with doctors to instruct the people in simple remedies.

He endeavoured to increase the wealth of the country by every means. He gave a concession to an Indian company to build a railway from Mecca to Jedda. He gave the Standard Oil Company of America permission to look for oil and others to look for gold or any minerals.

He increased the amount of land under cultivation by encouraging more and more bedouin to settle. Such settling meant water. He sent out experts to look for subsoil water and wherever it was found he built artesian wells.

Above all he gave the people peace and security. His rule was just and strong. He was quick to punish and he punished with severity. His prestige was supreme so that from end to end of Arabia his name was feared. He held the whole land firmly between his hands and he gave it stability such as it had never known in the history of man.

PART XV

CHAPTER LXXX

IBN SAUD is Lord of Arabia ruling by the force of his personality and the strength of his own right arm. An immense man, tremendous, vital, dominant. A giant thrown up out of the chaos and agony of the Desert—to rule.

The Desert, vast and brutal, demands extreme severity : a hand or foot lopped off for theft : a clan decimated for raiding : a head struck off for major crimes quickly and without formality.

Royal, majestic, and unperturbed Ibn Saud rules the Desert with justice and exemplary punishment. He has branded his will on the unruly people of his vast Empire.

He lives without pomp or ceremony. Sheik or slave, rich or poor, all have the right of audience before him : all are welcome as his guests. Sitting in his palace in Mecca or in his Audience Chamber in Riad, his plain Arab cloak drawn round him, his eagle face and his massive shoulders thrust forward as he receives his subjects, listens to their petitions and complaints, or gives terse orders to his officials, he might be one of the Great Caliphs.

He stands, basing himself four square on his trust in God, straddled across Arabia holding the whole land and its people between his clenched fists. He is inspired by a driving Belief —the Belief that he has been entrusted by God with a mission to knit all Arabs into one People, to lead them back to the greatness of their forefathers, and to make the Word of God Supreme.

THE END

WORKS CONSULTED AND GENERAL REFERENCES

BOOKS

AMEEN RIHANI : *Arabia Peaks and Deserts.*
Ditto : *Around the Coasts of Arabia.*
Ditto : *Ibn Sa'oud of Arabia.*
Ditto : *Molouk-al-Arab.*
Ditto : *Najd al hadith wa Mulhaqatuhu.*
AMIR ALI : *The Spirit of Islam.*
ARMSTRONG, H. C. : *Turkey and Syria Re-born.*
BELL, GERTRUDE : *Amuratt to Amuratt.*
Ditto : *The Desert and the Sown.*
Ditto : *Handbook of Tribes.*
Ditto : *Letters.*
BÉRARD, GÉNÉRAL EDOUARD : *Le Hedjaz de la guerre mondiale.*
Ditto : *Le Sultan, l'Islam et les Puissances.*
BOURGEOIS, ÉMILE : *Manuel historique de Politique étrangère.*
BROUCKE, JEANNE : *L'Empire arabe d'Ibn Seoud.*
BURCHARDT, J. L. : *Notes on the Bedouins and Wahabis,* 1831.
BURY, G. WYMAN : *Arabia Infelix.*
Ditto : *Pan Islam.*
CHEESMAN, MAJOR R. E. : *In Unknown Arabia.*
CHERADAME, ANDRÉ : *La Macédoine, Le Chemin de fer de Bagdad.*
CHIROL, VALENTINE : *The Occident and the Orient.*
COKE, RICHARD : *The Arabs' Place in the Sun.*
Ditto : *The Heart of the Middle East.*
DE LACY O'LEARY : *Arabic Thought and its place in History.*
DOUGHTY, C. M. : *Arabia Deserta.*
EDINBURGH CABINET LIBRARY, 1830 : *Popular Account of Arabia.*
ENCYCLOPÆDIA BRITANNICA, 12TH ED., VOL. XXXI.
GAULIS, MADAME G. B. : *La Question arabe.*
Ditto : *De l'Arabie du roi Ibn Sa'oud à l'Indépedence syrienne.*
GHERSI, E. : *Movimenti nazionalistici del mondo musulmano.*

GIBBS, H. A. R. : *Studies on Modern Arabic Literature.*
Ditto : *Whither Islam ?*
GRAVES, ROBERT : *Lawrence and the Arabs.*
HALDANE, SIR AYLMER : *The Insurrection in Mesopotamia.*
HARRISON, J. : *The Arab at Home.*
H.M. STATIONERY OFFICE : *Handbook on Arabia.*
HOGARTH, D. G. : *History of Arabia.*
Ditto : *Penetration of Arabia.*
HUART : *Histoire des Arabes.*
HUGHES : *Dictionary of Islam and Wahabis.*
HURGRONJE, C. SNOUCK : *Holy War made by Germany.*
Ditto : *Mekka.*
Ditto : *Revolt in Arabia.*
JACOB, H. F. : *Kings of Arabia.*
JUNG, EUGENE : *Les Puissances devant la revolte arabe.*
KAMMERER, A. : *Transjordania et l'Arabie.*
KOHN, HANS : *A History of Nationalism in the East.*
Ditto : *Nationalism and Imperialism in the Hither East.*
LAMMENS, H. : *Islam, Beliefs and Institutions.*
LANE-POOLE, S. : *The Mahommedan Dynasties.*
LAWRENCE, T. E. : *Revolt in the Desert.*
LECLERC, LÉON : *Histoire Contemporaire,* 1929
LODER, J. DE V. : *The Truth about Mesopotamia, Palestine and Syria.*
MACCULLUM, ELIZABETH P. : *Annual Survey of the Near East.*
MACPHAIL, SIR ANDREW : *Three Persons.*
MALMIGNATI, COUNTESS : *Through Inner Deserts to Medina.*
MARRIOTT, J. A. R. : *The Eastern Question.*
MELLONE, S. H. : *Western Christian Thought in the Middle Ages.*
MILIA, JEAN : *Visages Royaux.*
MITTWOCH : *Aus dem Yemen.*
MONTET, EDOUARD : *L'Islam.*
MOTT, J. R. : *The Moslem World of To-day.*
MUSIL, ALOIS : *Zur Zeitgeschichte von Arabien.*
NEWMAN, POLSON : *The Middle East.*
NICHOLSON, R. A. : *A Literary History of the Arabs.*
NIEBUHR, CARSTEN : *Voyage en Arabie.*
OFFICIAL HISTORY, VOL. II, *Egypt and Palestine.*
PALGRAVE : *Voyage en Arabie,* 2 vols. 1870.
PHILBY, H. ST. JOHN B. : *The Heart of Arabia.*
Ditto : *Arabia of the Wahabis.*
Ditto : *Arabia.*

PHILBY, H. ST. JOHN B. : *The Empty Quarter.*
PLOETZ : *Manual of Universal History.*
POWELL, E. ALEXANDER : *The Struggle for Power in Moslem Arabia.*
ROSSI, G. B. : *El Yemen, Arabia Felix o Regio Aromatum.*
RAUNKIAER, B. : *Through Wahabiland on Camelback.*
RUTTER, ELDON : *The Holy Cities of Arabia.*
SEKALY, ACHILLE : *Les deux Congrès Musulmans de* 1926.
SIRDAR IKBAL ALI SHAH : *Alone in Arabian Nights.*
SIMON, KATHLEEN : *Slavery.*
STODDARD, LOTHROP : *The New World of Islam.*
THOMAS, BERTRAM : *Alarms and Excursions in Arabia.*
   Ditto : *Arabia Felix.*
THOMAS, LOWELL : *With Lawrence in Arabia.*
TRITTON, A. S. : *The Rise of the Imams of Sanaa.*
WAVELL, A. J. B. : *A Modern Pilgrim in Mecca.*
WILLIAMS, KENNETH : *Ibn Sa'ud.*
WILSON, SIR ARNOLD : *Persian Gulf,* 1928.
   Ditto : *Loyalties.*
YOUNG, MAJ. SIR HUBERT : *The Independent Arab.*
ZWEMER, SAMUEL M. : *Across the World of Islam.*

NEWSPAPERS, PERIODICALS, TEXT-BOOKS, MAGAZINES, ETC.

Admiralty Handbook of Arabia.
American Geographical Society Journal, 1927 : " Arabia Deserta."
Annuaire du Monde Musulman.
Contemporary Review.
Cornhill Magazine.
Corriere Dela Sera.
Daily Telegraph, The.
Foreign Office Publications on Arabia, Peace Handbook No. 61 and paper 2566, Agreements with the Sultan of Nejd (Treaties of Haddah and Bahrah).
Frankfurter Zeitung.
L'Asie Française.
L'Europe Nouvelle.
L'Illustration.
L'Oriente Moderne.

Le Soir.
Le Temps.
Manchester Guardian.
National Review.
Nineteenth Century.
Report on Administration of Iraq, April 1922–March 1923.
Review of Civil Administration of Mesopotamia.
Revue du Monde Musulman.
Revue de Paris.
Royal Central Asian Society Journal.
Royal Colonial Institute Journal.
Royal Geographical Society Journal.
Royal Institute of International Affairs. Survey of International Affairs, and History of the Peace Conference.
Times, The
Umu-al-Kura

ROUGH MAP TO SHOW KING IBN SAUD'S CONQUEST OF ARABIA

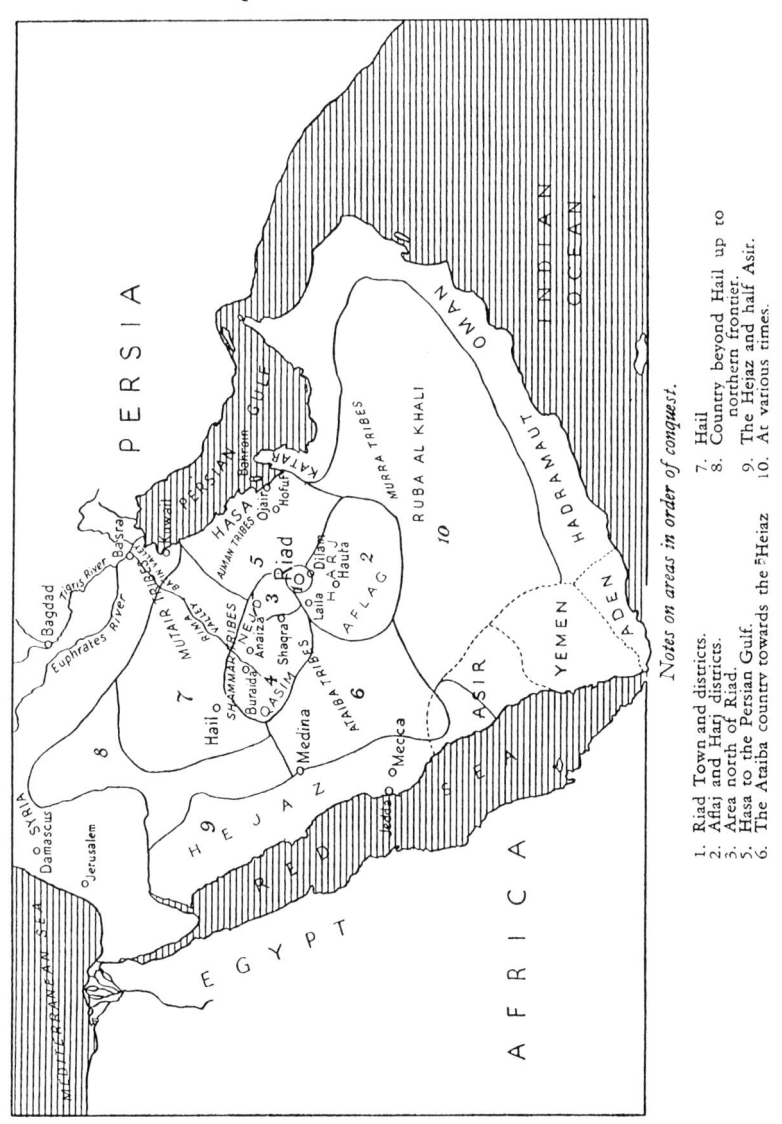

Notes on areas in order of conquest.

1. Riad Town and districts.
2. Aflaj and Harj districts.
3. Area north of Riad.
5. Hasa to the Persian Gulf.
6. The Ataiba country towards the Hejaz
7. Hail
8. Country beyond Hail up to northern frontier.
9. The Hejaz and half Asir.
10. At various times.

INDEX

A

ABDUL HAMID. (*See* Hamid, Abdul)
Abdul Wahab, the preacher. (*See* Wahab)
Abdullah (son of Husein Ibn Ali), 177-80, 186, 189, 203, 210, 211, 219, 221, 273
Ahmed (successor to Salim of Kuwait), 191
Ajlan (Governor of Riad under the Rashid), 53, 58, 59, 60
Ajman tribes, 95, 96, 104, 124, 125-36, 165 *et seq.*
Aleppo, 139
Ali (eldest son of Husein Ibn Ali), 220, 221, 224, 242
Allenby, General, 139, 141, 172
Anaiza, The people of, 90
Arab as opposed to European views and standards, 9
  Bureau in Cairo, The, 224
  Federations, Proposed, 121, 186
Arabia, Historical sketch of, 11-16
Artawiya, 113, 124
Ataiba, Country and tribes of, 95, 104, 159, 177, 192, 211
Aziz, Ibn Rashid, Abdul, 40 *et seq.*
  his conflict with and defeat by, Ibn Saud, 63-72
  description of, 84
  surprised by Ibn Saud, and killed, 85

B

BAGHDAD, 139
Basra, 81, 104
Belhaven, Lord, 141-6, 161, 162, 173
Bijad, Sultan Ibn (Sheik of the Ataiba), 219, 220, 225, 265, 270, 278
Britain, Great:
  determination to resist German projects in the East, 41, 42
  saves Mubarak and shuts one Eastern door against Germany, 47
  German designs against in the Persian Gulf, 77
  Germany's growing anger with, 117
  in the World War, 121 *et seq.*
  aids the hard-pressed Ibn Saud, 130
  Mesopotamian campaign, 139 *et seq.*
  subsidizes Husein of Mecca, 139-41
  smashing the Turks, 161
  conflicting policies of various Government Departments, 162
  intervenes between Ibn Saud and Husein, 177, 178
  holding the Arab countries together, 185
  Arab Confederacy plan, 186 *et seq.*
  Col. Laurence's obsession, 187
  troubles in Iraq, Egypt, India, and Turkey, 191-2
  Ibn Saud's threat to Palestine, 197, 198

Britain, Great (*contd.*):
 a lesson for the rash Ikhwan, 199
 terms of agreement with Ibn Saud, 202
 difficulties with Husein, 209
 pressure brought to bear on Ibn Saud, 235-7
Bulgaria, 172
Buraida (also town), Governor of, 91, 92, 130

C

CALIPH OF ALL ISLAM (TITLE CLAIMED BY HUSEIN), 211
Clayton, Sir Gilbert, 234, 257, 262, 271, 272
Committee of Union and Progress (Young Turk revolutionaries), 94
Cox, Sir Percy, 189, 200, 201, 204, 269

D

DAMASCUS, 109, 139, 141, 172, 182, 197, 219
Damascus to Medina Railway, 94, 141
Damluji (Saud's Foreign Secretary), 227, 245
Dawasir tribes, 124
Dawish, Feisal al (Sheik of Mutair), 91, 92, 104, 114, 162, 165, 167, 168, 192, 193, 203, 214, 233, 241, 252, 265, 266, 267, 268, 269, 270, 272, 278-81
Devil's Daughter, The (*i.e.* the Qasim), 83

E

EGYPTIAN ATTITUDE TO SAUD'S CONQUEST OF THE HEJAZ, 233
English, The. (*See* Britain)

European as opposed to Arab views and standards, 9
Execution of eighteen headmen at Laila, 96, 97

F

FADL, ABDULLAH AL, 257
Fadliya, Nafi Ibn, 156, 157
Fahad (son of Jiluwi), Governor of Buraida, 130, 153, 193
Feisal al Dawish.. (*See* Dawish)
Feisal (Ibn Saud's son), to rule the Hejaz, 255
Feisal (King of Iraq), 189, 192, 193, 203, 210, 219, 242, 252, 269
Fikri Pasha, 177

G

GERMANY:
 Eastern ambitions and the Constantinople to Baghdad project, 41, 42
 activities in the Persian Gulf, 77
 growing rage against Britain, 117
 the World War, 121 *et seq.*

H

HAFIZ PASHA (TURK GOVERNOR OF THE HASA), 33, 34
Hail, Capture of, by Ibn Saud, 194
Hamid, Abdul (the Sultan), 77, 94, 151
Hamza, Fuad, 257
Harb Arabs, 112, 113, 198, 199, 211, 255, 273, 286
Hasa, The, 105-107
Hazazina, The, 95, 96
Hejaz, The, 83, 94, 95, 211, 217, 225, 226, 227, 232, 243

Hithlain (Sheik of the Ajman tribes), 29, 126–36, 252, 265, 266, 272, 278, 281, 282
Hofuf, Capture of, by Ibn Saud, 104–107, 130, 131, 132
Husein, Ibn Ali (Governor of the Hejaz), 94, 95, 104, 109, 121, 122, 130, 139, 140, 142, 143, 158–69, 177–80, 186, 187, 189, 192, 193, 203, 205, 207–11, 215–23, 224, 233, 235

I

IDRISSI, HASAN, 286
Ikhwan tribes, 124 *passim*, 154, 162, 180, 197, 198, 199, 203, 212, 219, 220, 221, 224, 225, 232, 233, 239, 242, 256, 272–84
Indian Moslems, Attitude of, to Saud's conquest, 233, 234
Influenza plague, The great, 172
Iraq, 189, 192, 193, 203, 210, 211, 219, 266

J

JABIR (SON OF MUBARAK AND SHEIK OF KUWAIT), 136
Jarrid, Husein (Rashid, Governor of Qasim), 72
Jauhara (Ibn Saud's queen), Death of, 172–76
Jedda, 219, 221, 225, 226, 232, 241, 243
Jemal the Butcher (Governor of Syria), 140
Jews, The, 186, 187, 209
Jiluwi (brother of Ibn Saud), 32, 49, 51, 54, 55, 56, 57, 59, 60, 92, 93, 127, 279, 282, 283

K

KAISER, THE (WILLIAM II OF GERMANY), 41
Kanzan 129
Khurma, Town of, 159, 162, 164, 177, 179, 182, 205, 219
Kuwait, The Sheik of, 33, 34, 37 *et seq.*
   murdered by his brother Mubarak, 40
Kuwait. (*See also* the Sheik of):
   description of, 37–9
   becomes of world importance, 41 *et seq.*
   the key position in Central Arabia, 90
   raids into, 269

L

LAILA, TOWN OF, 95, 96, 97
Lawrence, Col. T. E., 140, 172, 187, 189, 209, 210, 224
Luwai (headman of Khurma), 179, 219, 220, 225, 228, 232, 265

M

MAUDE, GENERAL (IN MESOPOTAMIA), 172
Medina, 94, 140, 177, 207, 209, 219, 226, 233, 241, 255
Mecca, 94, 95, 140, 179, 180, 207, 208, 209, 215, 216, 219, 221, 224, 225, 226, 227, 231, 232, 242, 255, 256
Mohamed (Ibn Saud's son), 241
Mohamed, The coming of, 12 *et seq.*
Mosul, 172
Mubarak (brother of the Sheik of Kuwait), 40 *passim*

Mubarak (*contd.*):
  murders and succeeds his brother, 40
  sides with the English, 42
  his unorthodoxy and luxurious life, 43
  failure of his rise against the Rashid, 46
  saved by the English, 47
  intermediary between Ibn Saud and the Turks, 82
  turns against Ibn Saud, 90, 91
  more plotting, 104, 109
  abortive conference with Ibn Saud, 119
  declares for Britain in World War, 122
  aids Ibn Saud when hard pressed, 130
  his son Salim deserts Ibn Saud, 132
  replies to protest from Ibn Saud, 133
  his death, 134
Muklis Pasha (Governor of Basra), 82
Munasir pearl fishers, 105
Murra tribesmen, 31 *et seq.*, 99, 100
Mutair tribes, The, 91, 92, 104, 114, 124, 125, 203, 265, 268, 269
Mutib, Sad Ibn (Sheik of the Harb), 112, 113
Mutrif of Riad (Saud's standard-bearer), 193

N

NEJD, ONCE MORE UNDER A SAUD, 73, 91, 95, 194
Nura (sister of Ibn Saud), 81, 176

O

OBAID, IBN RASHID (COUSIN OF ABDUL AZIZ), 23

Obaid, Ibn Rashid (*contd.*):
  defeated and killed by Ibn Saud, 72, 73
Ojair, Port of, 127
Othman (Governor of Zilfi), 145

P

PALESTINE, 186
Peace Conference, 187
Persians and Saud's conquest of the Hejaz, 233
Philby, St. John, 141-6, 153, 161-4, 166, 174, 187
Pilgrimage to Mecca, The, 207, 255

Q

QASIM, THE (THE DEVIL'S DAUGHTER), 83
Qatar, The Sheik of, 31

R

RAHMAN, ABDUR (FATHER OF IBN SAUD), 16, 20, 21, 22
  his brothers Abdullah, Saud, and Mohamed, 22, 23
  efforts to free Riad, 25 *et seq.*
  Turkish offer of aid, 29-31
  claims protection from Murra tribesmen, 31 *et seq.*
  help from the Sheik of Kuwait, 33, 34
  another offer from the Turks, 37, 38
  disapproves of Mubarak's mode of living, 43
  joins his son after the capture of Riad, and is accepted as ruler, 64
  takes over the defence of Riad, 65

Rahman, Abdur (*contd.*) :
  negotiates with Turks on behalf of Ibn Saud, 82
  intercedes with the Wahabis, 90
  becomes a recluse, 112
  sends aid to Ibn Saud, 130
  still the adviser, 152
  welcomes his conquering son, 194
  anti-Husein conference at his house, 217
  death of, 272
Rashid, Abdul Aziz Ibn. (*See* Aziz, Abdul)
Rashid, Mohamed Ibn, 22, 23, 25 *et seq*
  death of, 40
Rashid, The (successor to Abdul Aziz), 123–5, 127, 130, 131, 165–71, 189, 191
Revolutionaries, Young Turk, 94
Riad :
  life there, 21, 22
  capture of by Rashid, 23, 25 *et seq.*
Rifada, Ibn, 273, 286
Rihani, Ameen, 231
Russia and Persian Gulf ambitions, 42
Ruwalla, The, 191, 197

S

SAD (BROTHER OF IBN SAUD), 95, 127, 129, 130, 131
Salim (a Sheik of the Shammar tribes), 23, 25, 26
Salim (son of Mubarak), 130, 132–34, 136, 158, 165, 166, 171, 189, 191
Saud, Ibn :
  pronunciation of name and descriptions, 9, 10
  birth of, 16
  his mother, 19
  his upbringing, 20, 21
  genealogical tree, 23

Saud, Ibn (*contd.*) :
  in the fighting to free Riad from the Rashid, 26 *et seq.*
  his brothers Mohamed and Jiluwi, 32
  becomes the complete bedouin, 33
  his marriage postponed through lack of means, 38
  life at Kuwait, 39
  abortive raid towards Riad, 41
  friendship with Mubarak, 40, 43
  meets foreigners and learns the art of ruling, 44
  failure of Mubarak's attack on the Rashid, 46
  inspired by Mubarak's defeat, and plans another raid on the Rashid, 49
  his wives, 49
  the raid on the Rashids, 50–2
  his bold capture of Riad, 55–60
  fortifies Riad and is joined by his father, 63, 64
  successful raids, 65, 66
  preparations for the crucial conflict with the Rashid, 67, 68
  he defeats the Rashid at last, 69, 70
  his position established, 71
  the two combatants compared, 71, 72
  his defeat and summary execution of Obaid Ibn Rashid, 72, 73
  Turkish designs against him, 77–83
  his diplomacy and spirit under defeat, 80
  another attack on the Rashid, 81
  his sister Nura, 81
  negotiations with the Turks, 82
  once more faces his enemy, the Rashid, 84
  surprise attack on the Rashid, who is killed, 85
  difficulties and dangers despite his successes, 89–91
  accident in fight with Shaminar tribesmen, 91

Saud, Ibn (*contd.*):
 defeats the Shaminar and the Mutair; and captures Buraida, 92, 93
 quarrel and "little peace" with Husein Ibn Ali, 95
 defeats his rebel cousins, and captures Laila, 96, 97
 consolidates his position, 99, 100
 his methods of dealing out justice, 101, 102
 capture of Hofuf and conquest of the Hasa, 104–7
 treaty with Turkey, 107
 new ambitions and policies, 108–14
 between two stools—Britain and Germany, 117, 118
 abortive conference with Mubarak, 119
 caught unprepared by the World War, 121
 negotiations with the English, 122–3
 severely defeated by the Rashid, 124, 125
 bluffs the Rashid and makes treaty with the English, 127
 flight after Ajman attack, 129
 fighting for his life, 130
 revenge on the Ajman, 131–6
 hit by a bullet, 132
 new marriage as a dramatic gesture, 133
 protests to Mubarak, 133
 supreme again in Nejd, 136
 receives mission from the English, 141–6
 price of neutrality, 142
 threat to Othman, 145
 a firm hand on his governors and sheiks, 146
 his life and appearance at the age of thirty-seven, 149–57
 quarrel with Husein, 158 *et seq.*
 failure to capture Khurma, 159
 in a cleft stick, 161 *et seq.*

Saud, Ibn (*contd.*):
 new campaign against the Rashid, 166–71
 death of his heir and his queen, 172–6
 views on adultery and fornication, 173, 174
 his marriages, 174, 175
 Husein's army routed, 177–80
 warned back by the English, 181
 alarmed by English attitude to him, 187–90
 bides his time and conquers Shammar country, 191–4
 proclaimed Sultan of Nejd and its Dependencies, 194
 conquest of the Ruwalla, 197
 his rash Ikhwan allies get a severe lesson, 199
 meeting with Sir Percy Cox, 200
 terms of agreement with Britain, 202
 dissatisfaction over conferences, 203, 204
 Husein captures Khurma and Turaba, 205
 attacked by erysipelas, 205, 206
 Khurma and Turaba regained, 207
 his old enemy Husein in a bad way, 207–11
 prepares to attack Husein, 211
 his practical zeal and faith, 212–15
 move to secure Moslem support, 217, 218
 campaign against Husein begins, 219–21
 Husein abdicates, 222, 223
 Husein's son appeals to the English, 224
 refuses Ali's peace move, 225
 becomes master of the Hejaz, 225, 226
 pilgrimage to Mecca, 227, 228
 sets up temporary administration, 231 *et seq.*
 beset by Moslem critics, 232–4

Saud, Ibn (*contd.*) :
gives way to English pressure, 235–6
determines to be King, 237–40
the last of Husein's family departs, 242
elected as King of the Hejaz, 243
calls a congress of Moslems, 245, 250
Moslem factions quarrel, 248, 249
agreement with the Yemen, 252
returns to Riad and is acclaimed King of Nejd, 253
establishes himself in the Hejaz, 254–8
difference between the Hejaz and the Nejd, 259–60
organises and strengthens his position, 261–2
recognised as King, 262
new dangers, 265–8
modern innovations, 261, 265, 266
asked to declare a Holy War, 266
compromises, 268
Mutairs attack the Iraqis and are bombed by the English, 269–70
protests to the English, 271
negotiations with Sir Gilbert Clayton, 272
troubles in the Hejaz, 273
the Great Assembly : success of his diplomacy, 274–7
quells the Dawish rebellion, 278–84
more innovations and organisation, 285–8
determines to be at peace with the English, 287
Saud (son of Ibn Saud), 257
Senussi, The Sheik of, 234
Shagra, Town of, 167
Shakespeare, Mr. (English Consul at Kuwait), 117, 118, 122, 123, 125
Shalan, Nuri (Sheik of Ruwalla), 191, 197
Shalub (Ibn Saud's chief steward), 153

Shamar tribes, The, 22, 28, 81, 86, 104, 121, 122, 124, 125, 165, 171, 191–4, 203
Suez Canal, The, 140
Suleiman, Abdullah al, 257
Syria, Arab Revolutionaries in 83, 94, 109, 110, 121, 122, 140, 186

T

TAIF, TOWN OF, 220, 221, 232
Tawil (Husein's Director of Customs in Jedda), 222, 224
Transjordania, State of, 189, 204, 211, 219, 273
Turaba, 179, 180, 181, 188, 205, 219, 221
Turaib razed by the Ikhwan, 199, 232
Turki (Ibn Saud's heir), death of, 172, 175
Turks, The, 29 *et seq.*
tools of Germany, 41 *et seq.*
they turn on Ibn Saud, 77–81
negotiations with the successful Ibn Saud, 82
plight of their garrisons in Curaiza and Buraida, 82
offer of gold to Ibn Saud and their withdrawal from Central Arabia 83
troops recalled owing to wars with Italy and Bulgaria, 104
yielding of Hofuf garrison to Ibn Saud, 106, 107
the World War, 121–3
help the Rashid to defeat Ibn Saud, 124, 125
in Mesopotamia campaign, 139 *et seq.*
plight of their armies, 161
thrust out of Arab countries, 172, 185
Caliphate abolished, 211

V

VERSAILLES, TREATY OF, 209

W

WAHAB, ABDUL (THE PREACHER), 13 et seq., 111, 164, 166, 215
Wahba, Hafiz (Saud's Egyptian counsellor), 219, 224, 227, 232, 245, 257, 283
Wahabis, The, 20, 89, 90, 105, 142, 159, 164, 165, 177, 212, 214, 217, 218, 221, 231, 232, 233, 239

Women:
 urge on combatants, 124
 kill the wounded, 135

Y

YAHA, IMAM (RULER OF YEMEN), 251, 252, 273, 287
Yasn, Usuf, 257
Yatraf, Beni, Shepherd tribes, 171
Yemen, The, 83, 94, 251, 252, 273
Yenbo, 226, 232, 241